PORTUGUESE STUDIES

Volume 32 Number 1
2016

Founding Editor
Helder Macedo

Editors
Catarina Fouto
Toby Green
Tori Holmes
Paulo de Medeiros
Paul Melo e Castro
Hilary Owen
Claire Williams

Editorial Assistant
Richard Correll

Production Editor
Graham Nelson

MODERN HUMANITIES RESEARCH ASSOCIATION

PORTUGUESE STUDIES

A peer-reviewed biannual multi-disciplinary journal devoted to research on the cultures, literatures, history and societies of the Lusophone world

International Advisory Board

DAVID BROOKSHAW	MARIA MANUEL LISBOA
JOÃO DE PINA CABRAL	KENNETH MAXWELL
IVO JOSÉ DE CASTRO	LAURA DE MELLO E SOUZA
THOMAS F. EARLE	MARIA IRENE RAMALHO
JOHN GLEDSON	SILVIANO SANTIAGO
ANNA KLOBUCKA	

Portuguese Studies and other journals published by the MHRA may be ordered from JSTOR (http://about.jstor.org/csp).

The **Modern Humanities Research Association** was founded in Cambridge in 1918 and has become an international organization with members in all parts of the world. It is a registered charity number 1064670, and a company limited by guarantee, registered in England number 3446016. Its main object is to encourage advanced study and research in modern and medieval European languages, literatures, and cultures by its publication of journals, book series, and its Style Guide. Further information about the activities of the Association and individual membership may be obtained from the Membership Secretary, Dr Jessica Goodman, St Catherine's College, Oxford OX1 3UJ, UK, email membership@mhra.org.uk, or from the website at: **www.mhra.org.uk**

Disclaimer: Statements of fact and opinion in the content of *Portuguese Studies* are those of the respective authors and contributors and not of the journal editors or of the Modern Humanities Research Association (MHRA). MHRA makes no representation, express or implied, in respect of the accuracy of the material in this journal and cannot accept any legal responsibility or liability for any errors or omissions that may be made.

Parts of this work may be reproduced as permitted under legal provisions for fair dealing (or fair use) for the purposes of research, private study, criticism, or review, or when a relevant collective licensing agreement is in place. All other reproduction requires the written permission of the copyright holder who may be contacted at rights@mhra.org.uk.

ISSN 0267–5315 (print) ISSN 2222–4270 (online)
ISBN 978-1-78188-256-6

© 2016 The Modern Humanities Research Association
Salisbury House, Station Road, Cambridge CB1 2LA, United Kingdom

Portuguese Studies Vol. 32 No. 1

CONTENTS

Preface	5
The Redactor of the Second Version of the *Chronicle of 1344*: Initial Traits for the Drawing up of a 'Facial Composite' ISABEL DE BARROS DIAS	7
The Subversion of Hate Literature in Anrique da Mota's *Farce of the Tailor* ANNA MATHESON	23
A Newly Discovered Novel and its Transnational Author: *Maria Severn* by Francisca Wood CLÁUDIA PAZOS ALONSO	48
Undone Anatomies: Femininity, Performativity and Parody in Mário de Sá-Carneiro's *A Confissão de Lúcio* ELEANOR K. JONES	62
'A fabulous speck on the Earth's surface': Depictions of Colonial Macao in 1950s' Hollywood RUI LOPES	72
Censored and Banned: Portuguese Films during the Government of Marcello Caetano (1968–74) ANA BELA MORAIS	88
Reviews	108
Abstracts	113

NOTES FOR CONTRIBUTORS

Articles to be considered for publication may be on any subject within the field but must not exceed 7,500 words, and should be submitted in a form ready for publication in English, sent as an email attachment to the Editorial Assistant at portuguese@mhra.org.uk.

Contributions whose standard of English is inadequate will be returned. Any quotations in Portuguese must be accompanied by an English translation. Submissions in Portuguese may be considered, but publication will be conditional on provision of a satisfactory translation at the author's expense. The Editorial Assistant may undertake translations on request for a reasonable charge.

Text and references should conform precisely to the conventions of the *MHRA Style Guide*, 3rd edn, 2013 (978-1-78188-009-8), £9.50, $19.00, €12.00, obtainable in print or online version from www.style.mhra.org.uk. All articles are subject to independent, anonymous peer review by experts in the field; authors receive written feedback on the editors' decision and guidance on any revisions required. *Portuguese Studies* regrets it must charge contributors for the cost of corrections in proof deemed excessive.

It is a condition of publication in this journal that authors of articles and reviews assign copyright, including electronic copyright, to the MHRA. Inter alia, this allows the General Editor to deal efficiently and consistently with requests from third parties for permission to reproduce material. The journal has been published simultaneously in printed and electronic form since January 2001. Permission, without fee, for authors to use their own material in other publications, after a reasonable period of time has elapsed, is not normally withheld. Authors may make closed-access deposit of accepted manuscripts in their academic institution's digital repository upon acceptance. Full open access to the accepted manuscript is permitted no sooner than 24 months following publication of the Contribution by the MHRA. Contributions may also be republished on authors' personal websites without seeking further permission from the Association, but no earlier than 24 months after publication by the MHRA.

Books for review should be sent to: Reviews Editor, *Portuguese Studies*, Dr Paul Melo e Castro, School of Modern Languages and Cultures, University of Leeds, Leeds LS2 9JT.

Preface

This issue of *Portuguese Studies* revolves around questions of identity, stretching in time from the Galician-Portuguese to Caetano-era censorship at the tail end of the *Estado Novo* and in space from the Iberian Peninsula to the South China Sea, raising important questions that continue to resound in contemporary debates.

In the first article, **Isabel de Barros Dias** puts forward her hypotheses concerning the second redaction of the *Crónica de 1344* in order to further our understanding of this important Galician-Portuguese text. She identifies three key characteristics — a Franciscan clerical bent, a didactic approach and a taste for courtly *topoi* — arguing that, while not giving us a name, these do give us at least an outline image of who the second redactor might have been. In the following article, **Anna Matheson** argues that Anrique da Mota's *The Farce of the Tailor* (c. 1500), rather than being — as first appears — a crude satire that lampoons a New Christian for his greed and his voluntary conversion from his ancestral religion, it is in fact a serious polemic on the subject of apostasy, and implicitly critiques Manueline policy towards his Jewish subjects in early sixteenth-century Portugal.

Drawing on careful archive work by which she re-discovered the book version of Francisca Wood's *Maria Severn* (1869), previously known only from its incomplete serial publication, **Cláudia Pazos Alonso** discusses this little-known novel set in Hampshire in terms of its commentary on Victorian England from a transnational perspective, widening our knowledge of its Portuguese author, her context and of cultural relations between Portugal and the United Kingdom in the second half of the nineteenth century. In her article, which shifts the focus south to Paris, and forward in time to the era of modernism, **Eleanor K. Jones** moves away both from traditional readings of Mário de Sá-Carneiro's *A Confissão de Lúcio* (1914) that underplay the novel's erotic charge and from more recent interpretations that have focused on the sexual tension between the male protagonists in order to focus on the author's treatment of his two female characters. Using Judith Butler's theorizations of gender, she argues for a radical re-thinking of his representation of their sexuality and gender identities.

The last two articles both deal with the increasingly important subject of film. Moving beyond Europe, yet remaining within the lusotopic space of the former Portuguese empire, **Rui Lopes** analyses the representation of Macao in 1950s American cinema, with a particular focus on *Macao* (1952), *Soldier of Fortune* (1955), and *Love is a Many-Splendored Thing* (1955). In line with other analyses of the way Portuguese colonial space has been represented in English, he discerns a tendency both to disparage Portuguese colonialism vis-à-vis the British Empire and to find it an exotic space where orientalist conventions and

Hollywood's hyperbolic sense of spectacle can be given free rein. In metropolitan Portugal, film, more than any other literary and artistic field, was subject to strict censorship from the inception of the *Estado Novo*. In her article, **Ana Bela Morais** focuses on the final years of the regime, under Marcello Caetano (late 1968 to 1974), using archive records to examine the attitudes of the censors towards Portuguese-made films, in particular. The detailed minutes of their discussions of what should be passed and what should be censored, restricted or suppressed provide a privileged insight into the institutional concerns of the regime and how attitudes to sexual and political content, in particular, were changing — or not changing — during the so-called Marcellist spring.

Finally, *Portuguese Studies* is pleased to resume, after a long absence, the publication of book reviews; it is hoped that this will become a regular feature of the journal. Authors and publishers wishing to send copies for review should refer to the details set out on page 4 of this issue.

THE EDITORS

The Redactor of the Second Version of the *Chronicle of 1344*: Initial Traits for the Drawing up of a 'Facial Composite'

ISABEL DE BARROS DIAS

Universidade Aberta and IELT / IEM (FCSH-NOVA), Portugal

The Portuguese *Chronicle of 1344* is a work that has stimulated much research and analysis, especially from the late twentieth century onwards.[1] The basis for these works is the meticulous study and textual edition prepared by Lindley Cintra in the 1940s and early 1950s.[2] The state of studies on post-Alfonsine chronicles in the first decades of the twentieth century compelled Cintra to focus on certain basic issues, at the cost of others, as he himself remarks in the Preface of the Introduction to his edition of the Chronicle:

> A Introdução que se vai ler é um estudo de história da cultura literária, não um estudo de história da literatura. Prepara este último mas não entra pelos seus domínios. Era necessário começar pelo primeiro, esclarecer os 'arredores' da Crónica antes de analisar o seu interior. Sem se saber

---

[1] Many articles have been published. PhD theses include Elisa Nunes Esteves, *Estudo Estético-literário: a Crónica Geral de Espanha de 1344* (Universidade de Évora, 1994), published as *A Crónica Geral de Espanha de 1344: estudo estético-literário* (Évora: Pendor, 1997); Maria do Rosário Ferreira, *A Lenda dos Sete Infantes: arqueologia de um destino épico medieval* (Universidade de Coimbra, 2005); and my own *Metamorfoses de Babel: a historiografia ibérica (sécs. XIII–XIV). Construções e estratégias textuais* (Universidade Aberta, 2000) published under the same title (Fundação Calouste Gulbenkian, 2003).

[2] Subsequently published by Luís Filipe Lindley Cintra, *Crónica Geral de Espanha de 1344* (Lisbon: IN-CM, 1951, 1954, 1961 and 1990); volume I corresponds to the study, and the other three to the critical edition. The *Crónica de 1344* is the Portuguese branch of the Iberian 'General Chronicles', a name used to designate the historiographical works written in vernacular under King Alfonso X of Castile, and other derived texts. Cintra has identified the main characteristics of the Portuguese branch, established its two main versions, the MSS that represent these versions, and has proposed Count Pedro Afonso de Barcelos as the author of the first version (of 1344). In the process of his scrutiny, Lindley Cintra also rearranged the relative position and dating of the various branches of Alfonsine and post-Alfonsine historiography, thus reshaping the general panorama of the ties between these several Iberian chronicles on the basis of their relationship with the *Crónica de 1344*. His findings and ideas were subsequently used and further developed by those working in this field. The appreciation of the innovative work of Lindley Cintra is already obvious in the first studies by Diego Catalán, especially his *De Alfonso X al conde de Barcelos* (Madrid: Gredos, 1962). Recognition of the value of his conclusions has also been backed by Catalán's disciples such as Inés Fernández-Ordóñez and Mariano de la Campa who, at present, continue the work of research and of textual edition of Alfonsine and post-Alfonsine historiographical works. Cintra's investigation has also been fundamental for all those scholars who have recently studied questions related to these historiographical works.

se se tratava de um original ou de uma tradução, se cada parte do texto era transcrição de uma obra anterior ou obra original do cronista, sem, numa palavra, identificar, caracterizar e situar a Crónica, era impossível realizar sèriamente a sua valorização como obra de arte. Neste trabalho preparatório me detive. (Cintra, *Crónica*, pp. xvii–xviii)

[...]

Não empreendi o estudo literário do texto. Não me chegou até agora o tempo para tanto. Tornada acessível a Crónica pela sua publicação, preparado o terreno pela Introdução, outros e eu próprio o poderemos empreender. (Cintra, *Crónica*, p. xviii)

[The following Introduction is a study of the history of literary culture, not a study of the history of literature. It prepares the grounds for the latter, but does not enter its realms. It is essential to begin with the history of literary culture to clarify the background of the Chronicle before examining its content. Not knowing whether it was an original or a translation, or if every part of the text was a transcription of an earlier work or the original work of the chronicler, in other words, without identifying, characterizing and situating the Chronicle, it was impossible to accurately assess its value as a work of art. I have focused on this preparatory work.

[...]

I have not undertaken the literary study of the text. So far, time has not allowed me to. Once I have made the Chronicle accessible through its publication and prepared the ground in its Introduction, others, and I myself, will be able to undertake this study.]

Although he edits the text of the second version of the *Chronicle of 1344*, Lindley Cintra focuses his study on its first version, an option that he justifies in the Preface:

Na edição, que me ocupou a maior parte destes anos, procuro reconstituir o texto primitivo da segunda redacção da Crónica, de fins do século XIV. Com os manuscritos até agora descobertos, é impossível chegar à reconstituição do texto de 1344. (Cintra, *Crónica*, p. xviii)

[In this edition, with which I have been largely engaged for the last few years, I try to reconstruct the original text of the second redaction of the Chronicle dating from the end of the fourteenth century. With the manuscripts that are presently available, it is impossible to reconstruct the text of 1344.]

Lindley Cintra's focus on the study of the first version of the *Chronicle of 1344* and its author meant that less attention was devoted to the second version, although it is obviously not forgotten. In fact, the reformulation of the Count of Barcellos' Chronicle is often in the background of the study, and sometimes we have passages specifically referring to it. This happens for instance when its original language — Portuguese — is confirmed (*Crónica*, pp. lxiv–lxxv) and when the main differences between the two versions are scrutinized (pp. xxxvi–xxxviii). Especially in the latter case we can find considerations regarding the extent of the interventions by the second redactor:

> Além disso, o segundo redactor preocupou-se em aperfeiçoar a expressão, procurou disfarçar as suturas entre a transcrição de fontes diversas, aspecto muito descuidado na redacção primitiva, particularmente no que respeita à *Crónica de Rasis*; retocou ou omitiu algumas frases e introduziu outras, de modo a adaptar a narração à sua particular concepção de estilo, o que conduziu a um maior afastamento das fontes; substituiu frequentemente o discurso directo pelo discurso indirecto; modernizou provàvelmente a língua. (Cintra, *Crónica*, p. xxxvi).

> [Furthermore, the second redactor was concerned with enhancing the expression; he sought to disguise the seams between transcriptions from different sources, an aspect that had been quite neglected in the earlier version, particularly when *Chronicle of Rasis* was used; he retouched or omitted some sentences and introduced others to adapt the story to his own concept of style, departing from the sources; he often replaced direct speech with indirect speech; he probably modernized the language.]

It is obvious that the second redactor's interventions had considerable depth, albeit to varying degrees throughout the chronicle. His alterations are particularly evident in the account of the earlier periods (roughly, the early days of the Reconquest and the preceding eras) since he used an Alfonsine source which was unknown to the Count of Barcellos.[3] In the account of later events, when the first version of the *Chronicle of 1344* already uses Alfonsine and post-Alfonsine texts, Cintra considers the intervention of the second redactor reduced:

> V) Desde o ponto em que o texto da primeira redacção da *Crónica* passa a ser uma refundição da *Crónica* de Afonso, o Sábio, o segundo redactor limita-se geralmente a fazer os retoques no estilo
> [...]
> VI) Como atrás ficou dito, é provável que, também na história dos reis de Castela posteriores a Fernando III, as alterações introduzidas se limitassem a arranjos da expressão (capítulos DCCCLVIII até fim). (Cintra, *Crónica*, p. xxxviii)

> [V) From the point in which the text of the first version of the chronicle becomes a recasting of the chronicle of Alfonso the Learned, the second redactor usually limits himself to enhancing the style
> [...]
> VI) As mentioned above, it is also likely that in the history of the kings of Castile who succeeded Ferdinand III, the alterations may have been limited to changes of style (from chapter DCCCLVIII onwards).]

Subsequent studies have focused on the texts of the two versions of the Chronicle and on the character of the Count of Barcellos.[4] The second redactor, until

---

[3] One of the main and most obvious differences between the first and second versions of the *Chronicle of 1344* is the fact that for the earliest periods of History the Count probably had no access to Alfonsine historiography, having used other sources, whereas the author of the second version reworked this textual block using Alfonsine sources.

[4] For a recent example of this trend see Georges Martin and José Carlos Ribeiro Miranda (eds), *Legitimação e linhagem na Idade Média peninsular: homenagem a D. Pedro, Conde de Barcelos* (Porto:

now, has been virtually forgotten. This is probably due to the fact that no clues about a specific individual have been found, unlike the case of Pedro Afonso of Barcellos, who was identified by Lindley Cintra as the most plausible author of the first version of the Chronicle (vol. I, parts III and IV). However, the absence of specific 'suspects' should not stop us from discussing this matter. We may not have an individual in mind, but we can identify a number of features that could help us to build the profile of the redactor of the second version of the *Chronicle of 1344*. To achieve our objectives, we have relied on existing evidence, the texts of the two versions of the Chronicle, and the Alfonsine and post-Alfonsine historiography of the textual families to whom its sources belonged.[5] The comparison between the two Portuguese versions is important for this research, but is often not possible, since our present knowledge of the first version is limited to the surviving manuscripts, which are truncated and fragmented. Besides, there are passages that cannot be compared; this happens whenever the two versions use different sources. Therefore, it is crucial to examine other related texts and especially, when possible, to scrutinize the attitude of the second redactor towards the non-Portuguese texts that he used.

The comparative analysis of these various versions confirms that the second version of the Portuguese chronicle should not be considered a simple ersatz, but a work with its own identity and charisma. Besides emphasizing some ideological and political traits already present in Count Pedro Afonso's work — particularly the pro-Portuguese attitude[6] — the second version carries a

Estratégias Criativas, 2011).

[5] For the Portuguese Chronicle, we have used, for the first version, the partial edition by Diego Catalán and María Soledad de Andrés (eds), *I edición crítica del texto español de la Cronica de 1344 que ordenó el Conde de Barcelos don Pedro Alfonso* (Madrid: Gredos, 1970) and the MS no. 2656 of the University Library of Salamanca (microfilm) — from now on **1344a**; and for the second version the critical edition by Cintra indicated in footnote 2 — from now on **1344b**. As for the Alfonsine and post-Alfonsine sources, we have used the various edited versions, choosing the ones suitable according to the passage under scrutiny: Ramón Menéndez Pidal (ed.) and Diego Catalán (reed.), *Primera Crónica General de España* (Madrid: Gredos, 1977) — from now on **PCG**; Inés Fernández-Ordóñez, *Versión crítica de la Estoria de España: estudio y edición desde Pelayo hasta Ordoño II* (Madrid: Fundación Ramón Menéndez Pidal / Universidad Autónoma de Madrid, 1993) — from now on **VC1**; Mariano de la Campa (ed.), *La Estoria de España de Alfonso X: estudio y edición de la Versión Crítica desde Fruela II hasta la muerte de Fernando II* (Málaga: Universidad de Málaga, 2009) — from now on **VC2**; Patricia Rochwert-Zuili (ed.), *Crónica de Castilla* (Paris: SEMH-Sorbonne — CLEA, 2010) — <http://e-spanialivres.revues.org/63> [accessed September 2014] — from now on **CrCast**; and Ramón Lorenzo (ed.), *La Traduccion Gallega de la Cronica General y de la Cronica de Castilla* (Orense: Instituto de Estudios Orensanos 'Padre Feijoo', 1975) — from now on **TradGall**. To determine which part of which edition was representative of which version (especially 'royal version' / 'primitive version', 'critical version', 'version of Sancho IV — 1289'), we have used mainly Inés Fernández-Ordóñez, 'La transmisión textual de la "Estoria de España" y de las principales "Crónicas" de ella derivadas', in idem (ed.), *Alfonso X el Sabio y las Crónicas de España* (Valladolid: Fundación Santander Central Hispano / Centro para la Edición de los Clásicos Españoles, 2000), pp. 219–60. For information on the sources used by the second version of the *Chronicle of 1344* we have relied especially on the data provided by Cintra (1951 — vol. I). In the quotations, all the underlinings are ours, as well as the translations.

[6] For a very simple example, in the Prologue of the 'royal version', we have a note pointing at the geographical limits of the matters that the chronicle deals with and that can be seen as a reflex of the concern about the Reconquest: 'et quales reyes ganaron la tierra fasta en el mar Meditarreneo;'

number of features that could be idiosyncratic, and therefore help us to make certain inferences and learn a little more about the profile of the person who composed this work.

Clerical Penchant

The second redaction of the *Chronicle of 1344* seems to be marked by a specific clerical penchant. This trait is not unusual for the late fourteenth century, since it seems to be in keeping with a specific religious movement that was particularly strong from the thirteenth century onwards, namely the mendicant model. In fact, some passages of the chronicle seem to exalt the ideal of worldly action, as opposed to monastic confinement. This reflects not only the mendicant mentality, but, more specifically, Franciscan values. The Franciscans were an important order in Portugal, and had a strong presence in various levels of society, including the aristocracy. Their influence on the royal court was notorious, especially that of Queen Saint Isabel (1271–1336; reigned 1282–1325)[7] and onwards. In fact, various elements of this order came to be in very close contact with political power as confessors and advisors to members of royal families, both in Portugal and in other kingdoms.[8]

(PCG, I: p. 4b). At the same point the second version of the *Chronicle of 1344* states 'e quantos e quaaes reys guaanharõ a terra da parte do mar Mediterreano e quaaes da parte do mar Ouciano' (II: p. 7), underlining thus that the scope of the chronicle extends also to the extreme west of the Peninsula. For a study that considers the ideological shifts of the Portuguese reworking of the Alphonsine materials, see Isabel de Barros Dias, *Metamorfoses de Babel: a historiografia ibérica (sécs. XIII-XIV). Construções e estratégias textuais* (Lisbon: Fundação Calouste Gulbenkian, 2003).

[7] Count Pedro Afonso of Barcellos was relatively close to Queen Isabel, since the illegitimate sons of King Dinis (including Pedro Afonso) were brought up in the court. The queen also took part in the negotiations that led to the second marriage of the count and he was by her side as she mediated in the truce between King Dinis and his son Afonso; see Cintra (*Crónica*, — vol. I: pp. cxxx–clxx — 'A vida do conde D. Pedro') and Frei Fernando Félix Lopes, OFM, *Colectânea de estudos de história e literatura*, 3 vols (Lisbon: Academia Portuguesa de História, 1997), in particular vol. III, pp. 223–38 ('Alguns documentos respeitantes a D. Pedro conde de Barcelos'). However we should not consider the possibility of attributing this clerical trend to the count, not least because the examples that we will give below are located in passages missing from Pedro Afonso's work.

[8] The Mendicants (and the Franciscans) were quite important and influential in Portugal from the thirteenth and fourteenth Centuries onwards, not only for their intellectual achievements and their influence as teachers and preachers, but also because of their presence in the court, having been counsellors and confessors of kings and queens of the first and second Portuguese dynasties. For more information on the Portuguese court of the fourteenth and fifteenth centuries, and the places occupied by ecclesiastics in this environment (functions, influence, etc.), see the chapter that discusses these questions in the book by Rita Costa Gomes, *A corte dos reis de Portugal no final da Idade Média* (Lisbon: Difel, 1995), pp. 108–29. See also the fundamental work of Frei Fernando Félix Lopes, OFM, *Colectânea de estudos de história e literatura*, 3 vols (Lisbon: Academia Portuguesa de História, 1997), in particular vol. II, pp. 407–60 ('Franciscanos Portugueses Pretridentinos — Escritores, Mestres e Leitores'), where the names and work of many Portuguese Franciscan intellectuals are indicated. See also: João Francisco Marques, 'Franciscanos e Dominicanos confessores dos reis portugueses das duas primeiras dinastias', *Revista da Faculdade de Letras — Línguas e Literaturas* — Anexo V: *Espiritualidade e Corte em Portugal. Sécs. XVI-XVIII* (Porto: Universidade do Porto, 1993), pp. 53–60 — online at <http://ler.letras.up.pt/uploads/ficheiros/artigo8031.pdf> [accessed Sept. 2014] — and the articles in *O Franciscanismo em Portugal* (Lisbon: Fundação Oriente, 1996), especially the articles by António Montes Moreira, 'Implantação e desenvolvimento da ordem franciscana em Portugal.

The following are several examples set in earlier times, but indicative of what would later be the Franciscan values and mentality. Above all, they seem to express quite clearly the idea of effective and active support to the weakest members of society. Absent from the first version of the Portuguese chronicle, these passages appear in its second version and are based on Alfonsine sources which are modified and adapted.

The first example is set in the reign of the Gothic King Reccared. The Portuguese text maintains the data extant in the Alfonsine historiography, which was already very laudatory of King Reccared, but it reworks the passage stylistically and provides more information. The new lines state that King Reccared recognized the exemplary and holy conduct of the bishops, their chaste words, their care of the poor, and distribution of alms from the coffers of the bishoprics. He also recognized how badly his father had treated the bishops when he exiled them and confiscated the rents that they so generously shared with the poor and the lepers. The charity and the devotion of the bishops to their flock continues to be highlighted in the second passage underlined in the quotation.[9] Thus, we are presented with an idealized portrait of the bishops of

---

Séculos XIII–XVI', pp. 13–27 (who provides an overview of the presence of Franciscans in Portugal); Humberto Baquero Moreno, 'O poder real e o franciscanismo no Portugal medievo', pp. 87–96 (who places the beginning of a well-defined royal favour of Franciscans under Kings Ferdinand and João I, which partially coincides with the timespan within which the second redaction of the *Crónica de 1344* was probably written, see p. 91); and Manuela Mendonça, 'O franciscanismo dos monarcas do século XV', pp. 139–52. For an overview of the presence and importance of Mendicants (and Franciscans) in the Iberian Peninsula, see the articles in Isabel Beceiro Pita (ed.), *Poder, piedad y devoción: Castilla y su entorno. Siglos XII–XV* (Madrid: Sílex, 2014), especially the articles by Francisco García-Serrano, 'Del convento al palacio: los frailes y las oligarquías castellanas (siglos XIII–XIV)', pp. 77–102 (on the rise to power of Mendicants and their proximity to kings and noblemen such as Don Juan Manuel); Isabel Beceiro Pita, 'La nobleza y las órdenes mendicantes en Castilla (1350–1530)', pp. 319–58 (on the closeness between these orders and the leading social groups in Castile); and Francesca Español, 'Formas artísticas y espiritualidad: el horizonte franciscano del círculo familiar de Jaime II y sus ecos funerarios', pp. 389–422 (on the 'philofranciscanism' of the Aragonese royal family at the end of the thirteenth century and start of the fourteenth).

[9] The two passages are as follows: '[...] el rey Recaredo seyendo muy manso et muy bueno et de grand plazer a todos, amauan le et preciauan le por ende, no tan solamientre los buenos, mas en uerdad aun los malos; e porque ell era muy franco et muy granado contra todos torno a los obispos et a la clerizia todos los thesouros et las cosas que el pudo saber que su padre tomara de las eglesias; e tan bueno fue et tan piadoso, que afloxo mucho a todos los pechos que a su padre solien dar et de las premias que les el solie fazer, e fazie muchas elmosnas a pobres et a lazrados, ca el tenie uerdaderamientre que pora esto le diera Dios el regno por que fiziesse y mucho bien et pora emendar los tuertos et las brauuras que su padre y fiziera' (PCG, I: 265a — chap. 477) and '[...] estando elle [Recaredo] em Tolledo, fazendo muyto ben e boo regimento ẽ seu reyno, assy como aquelle que era de muy boo siso e muyto amado de todos, por que lhes era muy franco e liberal, <u>ca veendo este rey Recaredo o boo exemplo do sancto vyver dos bispos e a sua muy casta e limpa cõversaçom e como avyam grande cuydado dos pobres e lhes mynistravã cõ maravylhosa diligencia as esmollas daquellas rendas que avyam dos bispados, fez conciencia do mal que seu padre fezera em desterrar os bispos e clerigos de tam sancta entẽço e de lhes tomar as rendas que elles com tanto fervor destrebuyam aos lazerados.</u> E, por esto, tornou aos bispos todallas rendas que lhes seu padre tomara; <u>ca certamente os bispos que erã aaquella sazõ erã de tam fervente carydade que todallas rendas erã dadas aos mesteyrosos e elles prestes pera poer suas almas por seus subditos.</u> E tanto foi este rey de dereyta entençom que elle alyvou o poboo muyto das peytas que a seu padre sohyam de dar e das premas que lhes elle soya fazer. Este amava muyto os proves e fazialhes muytas esmollas, ca elle ẽtẽdya que por esso lhe dera Deus o reyno, por que fezesse em elle todo ben e ẽmendasse os tortos e crueldades que seu padre avia feytas' (1344b, II: 203–04 — chap. 134).

that time, extolling their benevolence towards the poor, the weak, and the sick.

The second example is an amplification of a passage praising Saint Ildefonso. In the Alfonsine text, this saint was commended for his intellectual works, and his rhetorical and preaching skills. In the Portuguese text, these qualities are complemented with a reference to his exemplary life and his assistance to the poor.[10]

This passage also provides information that leads us to disregard the possibility of a Dominican trend. These friars, whose intellectual profile was more marked, also had a very important cultural presence in Portugal where their main scope of activity seems to have been in juridical and ecclesiastical matters, political intervention, teaching, and, first and foremost, preaching. Given the importance this order gave to rhetoric and evangelization, if the person who reworked the *Chronice of 1344* was a Dominican (or a layman sympathetic with this order), he certainly would have emphasized the preaching and writing capacities of Saint Ildefonso. Instead, he stresses his actions in helping the poor.

However, in the 1380s and 1390s, at the height of the rift within their order between 'Observantes' and 'Claustrais', the Franciscans considered worldly actions a priority. The reformist party, or Observantists, particularly viewed poverty as fundamental in observing the Franciscan Rule, which is precisely the question raised in the two examples provided.[11] This brings us to a third example, a portrayal of Saint Isidore, in which more general qualities are

---

[10] The two passages are as follows: 'Este sant Alffonsso fizo muchos libros et muchos escriptos buenos ante que fuesse arçobispo, et despues que lo fue otrossi, e algunos daquellos escriptos fincaron a su muerte que non fueron acabados. E por que la gracia de Dios onrrara la su boca de buena palabra, e porque la fe de Cristo fue confirmada et raygada en toda Espanna et en la Galia Gotica por libros que el fiziera de la uirgindad de sancta Maria et dotras cosas buenas muy apuestas et de fremosas palabras, llamauan le todos por ende «sant Alffonso boca doro».' (PCG, vol. I: p. 283a — chap. 511). and 'Sant'Ilafonso, seendo arcebispo de Tolledo, fez muyto ben, ca todas as rendas que elle avya erã muyto humildosamente destrebuydas aos pobres, en tanto que elle e os que o serviam escassamēte avyam o mantiimēto e o vestido. Este era muy devoto de Sancta Maria. Este fez muytos e boos livros, assy ante que fosse arcebispo como depois que o foy. Elle avya muy doce pallavra em preegar e muy fremoso exemplo ẽ vyver, en tal guysa que elle, assy na vida como na preegaçom, seguya muyto a doutrina dos apostollos e o exemplo de Jhesu Cristo, ca elle aprēdera de seu meestre Sancto Isidoro seer mansso e homildoso e pobre de coraçon. E tanto avya fremosa e faagueira pallavra em preegar, que os que o ouvyam eram muy confortados e confyrmados ēna fe. Elle tirou de toda a Espanha o error da virgiindade de Sancta Marya e ainda em a Gallya Gotica. Este, ennos livros que fez, seguyo tan fremosa rectorica e cōpoymento de pallavras que lhe chamaron Sant'Ilafonso, boca d'ouro.' (1344b, vol. II: pp. 228–29 — chap. CLIV).

[11] I thank Professor José Mattoso for the information on the opposition between 'Claustrais' and 'Observantes', as well as for recommending his article on 'O tempo de Santa Beatriz da Silva', in José Eduardo Franco and José Sanches Alves (eds), *Santa Beatriz da Silva: uma estrela para novos rumos* (Cascais: Principia Editora, 2013), pp. 23–37 where the historical context before the sixteenth century is outlined: the plagues, wars and famines, as well as the crises in the Catholic Church that stimulated the emergence of reform movements such as the 'Observantes' in the Franciscan order. I also thank Professor Mattoso for having read and commented on this article. The specific context of the final decades of the fourteenth century is also outlined by Francisco da Gama Caeiro, 'A cultura portuguesa no último quartel do século XIV', in *Actas do ciclo de conferências Aljubarrota 600 anos* (Lisbon: Sociedade Histórica da Independência, 1987), pp. 367–87, stressing not only the problems of the period, but also the remarkable contribution of Franciscans to the coeval Portuguese culture.

referred to (evangelization, honesty, frugality, joy, humble dress, etc.). This passage is eloquent because it stresses not only the need to attend to the poor, but also, following the example of Jesus Christ, to pursue a life of poverty and humility and take a stand against vainglorious clerics.[12] This passage also includes a reference to assisting widows and orphans, a cliché of chivalric romances, and a question that will be discussed later on in this article.

Admittedly, this information could have already been in the particular manuscript used by the author of the second version of the *Chronicle of 1344*, or in some additional source that he might have handled. However, the latter seems unlikely because this type of source usually provides extra information on a specific point, while the Franciscan trend shows up consistently in different places throughout the narrative. The possibility that this is a penchant already conveyed in the basic source manuscript is a valid hypothesis, especially because King Alfonso X also had Franciscan collaborators, such as Juan Gil de Zamora,[13] but we lack information to verify it because we do not know exactly which manuscript it was.[14] In view of the available data, the most plausible

---

[12] 'Este era muy graado em dar as esmollas <u>aos pobres e muy aprestes pera os receber</u> con grande alegria; e era muy verdadeyro ẽna sentença que dava e dereito ẽ todo seu juizo; e era de grande fervor e muy avyvado ẽ preegar a pallavra de Deus <u>e era muy cõforme aa proveza e humildade de Jhesu Cristo e de todos seus feitos muy devoto</u>. Este era de grande trabalho e muy agudo em despoer a escriptura e muy diligẽte em guaanhar as almas pera Deus; e era muy honesto e temperado em comer e muy homildoso ẽno vestyr, <u>ca dizia elle que nõ era razon que os bispos, que devyã seer servos de Jhesu Cristo, fosem vestidos de pomposas vestiduras, ca nõ era o servo mayor que sey senhor</u>. Este era mui paciente e alegre em as tribulaçoões e devoto em sua oraçon e sempre era desejoso de seer martyr por amor de deffender a fe de Jhesu Cristo. Este era enssynador de clerigos e muy fremoso eixẽplo aos frades e freyras, consolador dos que choravam, <u>grande deffendymẽto das vyuvas e criador dos orffoõs e quebrantador dos sobervosos clerigos</u> e persiguydor dos escomungados herejes e conhecedor dos ipocritas.' (1344b, II: 215–16 — chap. 145). In turn, the same passage in *Estoria de Espanna* says the following: 'Este sant Esidro [...] et muy granado en dar elmosnas, acucioso pora reçebir huespedes, alegre de coraçon, verdadero en la sentencia que daua, derechero en el iuyzio, auiuado en predigar, en su castigo de buen donario, e en ganar almas a Dios muy agudo, en esponer la Sancta Escripyura atemprado, en el conseio que daua muy prouechoso, en su uestir omildoso, en comer sofrido, en la oracion deuoto, siempre appareiado pora morir por deffendimiento de la uerdad esto es Dios, en todos sus fechos muy onesto. Sin esto, era padre de los clerigos, maestro et mantenedor de los omnes dorden et de las mugieres, consolador de los cuytados et de los que llorauan, amparador de los pobres e de las bibdas, alliuiamiento de los muy cargados, deffendedor de los suyos, crebantador de los soberuios, perseguidor et maltraedor de las heregias et de los hereges.' (PCG, I: 277a — chap. 500).
[13] It is possible to point out a number of Mendicant friars who were involved in the writing of History, both in regard to their congregation, and of a more general scope. Juan Gil de Zamora, collaborator in the historiographical works of Alfonso X, is a good example of this. We can also mention the case of Fra Salimbene da Parma and of Fra Paolino di Venezia, in Italy, besides the many friars involved in the composition and translations of the Chronicles of their order. There are also examples of Dominicans who engaged in the writing of historiographical works, such as Vincent of Beauvais or, in Portugal and at a far more modest scale, Frei Afonso de Alfama, who wrote *Breves crónicas*. Nevertheless, this seems not to be their fundamental trend of intervention — see Saul António Gomes, 'Os dominicanos e a cultura em tempos medievais: o caso português', *Biblos*, 7 (2009), 261–94. Gomes studies the action and the literary activity of Dominican Portuguese scholars, who seem to have mainly written sermons, lives, encyclopaedic works, commentaries, etc.
[14] Diego Catalán, *De la silva textual al taller historiográfico alfonsi: códices, crónicas, versiones y cuadernos de trabajo* (Madrid: Fundación Ramón Menéndez Pidal / Universidad Autónoma de Madrid, 1997), seconded by Inés Fernández-Ordóñez, 'La transmisión textual' (pp. 258–59), says that

hypothesis seems to be that the additions were made by the redactor of the second version of the *Chronicle of 1344* and were therefore in line with his own values.

Didactical Inclination

The second penchant that we have identified is also in keeping with Mendicant ideas, since these coincide with the didactical aspect of historiography. There is a clear tendency to fully transcribe, or to develop pieces of advice similar to the *Specula principorum*, a genre widely practised by Mendicant authors, and by Franciscans.[15] This genre has a long and ancient tradition. One of its peaks occurs in the thirteenth and fourteenth centuries, mainly due to the success and dissemination of works written in the French court circle (John of Salisbury, Vincent of Beauvais, Thomas Aquinas, Giles of Rome, among others).[16] The Iberian Peninsula was not unaffected by this trend. The Portuguese Franciscan Álvaro Pais (c. 1275–1349) was the author of a *Speculum regum* (1341–44) dedicated to Alfonso XI of Castile.[17] Giles of Rome's (c. 1243–1316) *De regimine principum* (c. 1287) was known in the fourteenth century in Spain, where it was translated into Castilian and commented on by Juan García de Castrojeriz, c. 1344. This work influenced several Castilian authors, as evidenced in a reworking of the *Castigos del rey don Sancho IV*,[18] and in an earlier allusion made by Don Juan Manuel.[19]

---

after the kingdom of Alaricus, the second version of the *Chronicle of 1344* changes source. First it uses a testimony of the 'primitive version' and then begins to use a testimony of the 'critical version'. The examples presented here are part of this latter section. Unfortunately there is no edition of the 'critical version' for this period and we are therefore unable to assess the changes in relation to this textual family. Besides, no particular manuscript has been identified as a possible source for the Portuguese chronicle.

[15] On the closeness between preaching and teaching (as a way to convey specific ideas and spirituality) see the article by Francisco da Gama Caeiro, 'Ensino e pregação teológica em Portugal na Idade Média: algumas observações' *Revista Española de Teología*, 44 (1984), 113–35. See also, by the same author, 'A cultura portuguesa no último quartel do século XIV', where a change in literary taste is noted: the decadence of lyric poetry and the emergence of moral, mystic and didactical prose, as well as of chivalry romances (pp. 381–84). On the convergence between *specula* and the second redaction of the *Chronicle of 1344*, see Isabel de Barros Dias, 'Modelos teóricos e descrições aplicadas: imagens de soberanos na cronística ibérica de inspiração afonsina (sécs. XIII–XIV)', in Ana Sofia Laranjinha and José Carlos Ribeiro Miranda, *Modelo. Actas do V Colóquio da Secção Portuguesa da Associação Hispânica de Literatura Medieval* (Porto: Faculdade de Letras da Universidade do Porto, 2005), pp. 117–28.
[16] For a general idea on these authors and their works, see the contextualizing chapter in Ana Isabel Buescu, *Imagens do Príncipe: discurso normativo e representação, 1525–49* (Lisbon: Cosmos, 1997). See also the article by David Nogales Rincón, 'Los espejos de príncipes en Castilla (siglos XIII-XV): un modelo literario de la realeza bajomedieval', *Medievalismo*, 16 (2006), 9–39.
[17] On this author, see António Domingues de Sousa Costa, *Estudos sobre Álvaro Pais* (Lisbon: IAC, 1966) and João Morais Barbosa, *Álvaro Pais* (Lisbon: Verbo, 1992).
[18] For more information, see the article by Hugo O. Bizzarri, 'Notas para la edición de un Regimiento de Príncipes', *Memorabilia*, 3 (1999) online at <http://parnaseo.uv.es/Memorabilia/M4/Bizzarri3.htm> [accessed Sept. 2014].
[19] On this question see Hugo O. Bizzarri, 'El concepto de ciencia politica en don Juan Manuel', *Revista de Literatura Medieval*, 13.1 (2001), 59–77.

The final example presented above referred to the aspiration to behave like Christ. The 'mirrors for princes' follow the same logic since they are ethical guides that present ideal images of sovereigns (their expected virtues, duties, how to behave towards the church, the kingdom and their subjects), as examples to be followed.[20] Its aims converge with those of chronicles in so far as these can be seen in the light of the *magistra vitae*, the Ciceronian ideal of history, a purpose expounded in Alfonso X's historiography and accentuated in later versions. It is possible that during his exile in Castile, Pedro Afonso de Barcellos had come into contact with the popular literary genre of the *Specula principorum*. In fact, we cannot help noticing that in the speech that the dying Count Henry of Portugal addresses to his young son, Afonso Henriques, the text of the second version of the *Chronicle of 1344* matches that in the *Lineage book* of Count Pedro.[21] This means that in this case either we cannot attribute it to the second redactor, or we will have to consider the hypothesis that someone reworked both the works of the Count.[22] This passage of advice also occurs in the 'critical version' (CV2: pp. 560-61 — chap. CCCLXIX) and quite similarly, since the main difference that is evident in the two Portuguese texts is the addition of the final phrase of the speech.[23]

Another example can be found in the second version of the Chronicle, in which a piece of advice is clearly extended. This passage has the advantage of being reported in several texts, thus allowing for a more ample comparative analysis. It takes place when Ferdinand I divides his kingdom among his sons. In the 'critical version', the king identifies the several regions of his kingdom, comments on its population and curses any of his sons who might dare to challenge the division he has established (VC2: pp. 416-21 — chaps CCXXXVII-CCXXXVIII). The same episode is summarized in the 'version of

---

[20] For an insight on the presence of *specula* and the importance of examples in education and in the readings of kings and nobles see the articles by Isabel Beceiro Pita, *Libros, lectores y bibliotecas en la España medieval* (Murcia: Nausícaä, 2007) about the education, the culture and the libraries of Iberian nobility.

[21] José Mattoso (ed.), 'Livro de Linhagens do Conde D. Pedro', in *Portugaliae Monumenta Historica — Nova Série* (Lisbon: Academia das Ciências, 1980), vol. I, title VII, pp. 123-24.

[22] This hypothesis is tempting. In the Introduction to the edition of the Lineage Book, José Mattoso considers that the person who reworked this text c. 1382 has made changes in title VII, although he doesn't specify what these changes were (p. 43). He also states: 'As suas propensões literárias levaram-no a refundir também outras narrativas de carácter mais romanesco' (p. 44), which matches the third trait presented here.

[23] The text in the second redaction of the *Chronicle of 1344* is as follows: '- Filho, toda a terra que eu leixo, que he des Estorga ataa Leõ e ataa Coimbra, non percas della nẽ hũa cousa, ca eu a tomey cõ muyto trabalho. Filho, toma esforço do meu coraçõ e sey semelhavel a mỹ. E sey companheiro aos fidalgos e dalhes todos seus dereitos. E aos cõcelhos fazelhes hõrra. E faze de guisa que todos ajam dereyto, assy os grandes como os pequenos, e por rogo nẽ por cobiiça, nõ leixes de fazer justiça. E porem, meu filho, sempre em teu coraçõ ama justiça, ca o dia que a leixares de fazer hũu palmo, logo o outro dia ella se afastara de ty hũa braça. E porem, meu filho, am a justiça e averas a beençõ de Deus e a graça e bemquerença das gentes. E non consentas os teus homẽs seer sobervosos e atrevidos em mal fazer nem façam força a nehũu, ca perderias o teu boo preço se taaes cousas nõ castigasses.' (1344b: IV, 215-16 — chap. DCCV).

Sancho IV — 1289' (PCG: pp. 493b-94b — chap. 813)[24] where King Ferdinand exhorts his sons to keep the land he leaves them and not to fight against each other. He establishes no further rules of conduct except that he counsels them to follow the Cid's advice. In the *Galician translation* the episode is even more synthesized (TradGall: pp. 348-49 — chap. 205-06): the three kingdoms are presented and the king hands over the Cid to his son Sancho, without any suggestion that he should follow his vassal's advice. In the *Crónica de Castilla*, no advice or suggestions are mentioned (CrCast, I: chap. 28). The manuscript of Salamanca, with the first version of the *Chronicle of 1344*, is considerably damaged at this point. However, it already mentions some questions elaborated in the second version.[25] This last text, while mainly summarizing matters, changes tack and develops the passage on the advice that the old King Ferdinand gives to his sons as he is dying:

> — [...] Porẽ vos rogo, meus filhos, que sempre vos ajades bem cõ os fidalgos das vossas terras, fazendolhes sempre bem e mercee, e outrossi a todollos outros homẽes que vollo forem demãdar, ca nõ cõvem aos reis seer de avarẽtos corações. E esto meesmo fazede aos pobres das vossas villas e cidades. Amade os vossos poboos nõ lhes fazendo sem razon, ca todos me serviron mui bẽ e ajudarõ a guaanhar a terra que a vos outros fica. Seede sesudos e temperados, muy sofrudos e esforçados nas batalhas, e muy francos em partyr vosso aver. Seede mesurados e de boa palavra e bem recebentes. Honrrade os estrãjeiros. Seede muy verdadeiros, castos e temperados e fiees catholicos, filhos obedientes na santa fe do Nosso Senhor Jhesu Cristo. Deffendede bem vossos reinos aos mouros e tomade os seus. E amadevos todos tres e avede paz e cõcordia (1344b: III, 346-47 — chap. CDLXXII)

> [— [...] Therefore I entreat you, my children, to always maintain good relations with the noblemen of your lands, favour them and do them well, and the same with every other man who turns to you, because kings should not be avaricious of heart. And do the same to the poor in your towns and cities. Love your people and do them no harm, because they have all served me well and helped me win the land that I now leave you. Be serious and temperate, most diligent and engaged in battle, and always liberal with the division of your possessions. Be restrained, true to your word, and welcoming. Treat foreigners honourably. Be correct, chaste, and temperate and faithful Catholics, obedient sons in the holy faith of our Lord Jesus Christ. Defend your kingdom from the Moors, and take theirs. All three of you love each other and preserve peace and harmony.]

[24] See Inés Fernández-Ordóñez, 'La transmisión textual', p. 243 — pp. 429a to 565a of PCG (corresponding to fols 82-198 of the Royal manuscript E2) convey the 'amplified version of 1289'.
[25] 'Et dixo a sus fijos a don Sancho a vos finca el rreyno de Castilla a don alfon a vos finca el rreyno de leon a don garcia a vos finca el rreÿno de gallicia con todo lo al [que(?)] gané en portogal e porende rreÿne ... cada uno de vos mis fillos .... fagades a vros(?) [= vuestros(?)] cavalleros et a los con ... res ... eños et alos vros(?) [=vuestros(?)] fydalgos delos vras(?) [=vuestros(?)] reynos(?) como(?) los .... co ... os dernd a [ordenades(?)] vrosos(?) [vuestros(?)] rreynõs fuere .... dre quando vos lo fuere a demandar et esso mesmo alos pueblos de las vras(?) [=vuestras(?)] villas et cibdades de..d.. no de vos ca todos me fizieran(?) muy bien et me ayudaron a gañar mujas villas et mũjos castillos a .... de vos enlos rreynos que vos fincan et ellos dixeron que ansi lo fazrjan' (1344a: fol. 216$^{r\,a-b}$ — chap. 369).

Two other examples of this didactical trend occur during the rule of the Goths. The first one is an amplification of recommendations given by King Leonagildo to his son, when he repents for the all the evil he is guilty of, having persecuted followers of the Catholic faith, and asks his son to atone for his wrongdoing.[26] The second one consists of the advice of King Teudorigo to his grandson, Amalarigo, when he decides that the young man can assume control of the Spanish kingdom. In the Alfonsine 'royal version', there is a brief note in which the old king advises his grandson to always maintain good relations with Rome and its Emperor.[27] In the second version of the *Chronicle of 1344*, we find that the passage is modified and expanded, referring a wide number of suggestions about how a good sovereign should behave.[28]

Didacticism is a transversal characteristic of many texts produced in the Middle Ages, and it would not be a remarkable feature *per se*, if not for the fact that the second version of the *Chronicle of 1344* recurrently reworks and expands passages where advice is provided or referred to.

---

[26] '— Meu filho, sabee que eu som acerca de mynha morte, a qual eu ben mereço por os meus pecados, ca eu matey meu filho Hermenegildo por a lealdade da sua fe, persseguy e matey e desterrey muytos nobres e fiees catholicos cristaãos. Por que vos rogo que, aquello que eu mal fige, que vos o corregades, se vos Deus der estado de rey, e que mandees por Mãsona e por Leandre, arcebispos, e por todolos outros que eu desterrey; e tornadeos cada hũu a seu logar. E rogovos que creades estes arcebispos, Mansona e Leandre, assy spiritualmente como no temporal, por que son homeẽs de grande santidade e muy provados na sua fe, e os ajudes por padres e obedeeçades a todos seus castigamẽtos.' (1344b, II: 199 — chap. 131). The passage in the *Estoria de Espanna* is far more plain: 'enfermo Leouegildo en Toledo duna grand enfermedad, e mando a su fijo Recaredo que enuiasse por los arçobispos que el desterrara et que los tornasse a sus logares: a sant Leandre a Seuilla, e a sant Ffulgencio su hermano a Ecija, e a Mausona a Merida, e que los oyesse et los creyesse de lo quel dixiessen como a padres, et que obedesciesse los castigamientos dellos.' (PCG, I: 263b — chap. 473). The passage is absent from 1344a.

[27] 'pues que el rey Theoderigo uio que Amalarigo su nieto era llegado a edad para mantener aquel regno de las Espannas que el tenie por el, diogele, et fizol ende rey et sennor et quel ouiesse entrell et su fija desse Theoderigo en toda su uida. [...]. Et coniurolos el rey muy fuert et mandoles por mandamientos que amassen siempre al senado et al pueblo de Roma, et que punnassen de auer por amigo all emperador quanto ellos mas pudiessen. Pues que esto les ouo dicho, tornosse el pora tierra de Italia,' (PCG: I, 250 — chap. 443).

[28] '— Meu filho, vos sodes em tal ydade que ja saberedes reger reyno; e porẽ eu querovos dar os reynos que foron de vosso padre. E comprevos saber as condiçõoes que deve aver o rey: ca o rey deve seer sabedor, franco, liberal e nobre de coraçom; deve de seer acustumado, tenperado e ygual a todos, justiçoso e boo governador e seer sem cobiiça senom de honrra e de senhorio e seer de muy boo consselho e muy forte e esforçado ẽnas batalhas e amador do seu poboo e acrecentador de sua terra. Porẽ vos rogo, meu filho, que aprendades esto que vos digo e que ajades sempre ẽ vosso consselho homẽes de boas conciẽcias e sabedores e fidalgos e boos conselheiros e de grandes coraçõoes, ca taaes compre ao rey aver em seu conselho, por que, quando lhes demandar conselho em os grandes feitos, que lho possam e saybam dar. Nunca cheguedes a vos e a vosso conselho homẽes de baixo sangue e vyl condiçon, ca taaes como estes nom ham bõo conselho em feyto d'armas nem som pera grandes feytos, ca estes nõ sabem consselhar os reys senom ẽ tirãnya do poboo e desavenças dos fidalgos e todos maaos costumes e esto por fazerem de sy grandes e ricos, a qual cousa elles nõ ham de sua natureza; ca nom pode o rey aver mais perigosos ẽmiigos que maaos conselheiros. Grande myngua he ao rey cõverssar com homẽes viis. E porende vos, meu filho, regeevos segundo o que vos hey devysado. E prezade e hõrrade os fidalgos. E amade e regede bem os poboos. E a todos geeralmente fazede dereyto e justiça e assy seeredes amado e temudo. Outrossy vos mando que amedes sempre o senado e o poboo de Roma e que ajades por amygo o emperador' (1344b, II: 168–69). The passage does not occur in 1344a.

Taste for Books of Chivalry

A third penchant that might be attributable to the redactor of the second version of the *Chronicle of 1344* is a taste for romances. This trend shows up in certain *topoi* that are common in texts of this genre and that are reproduced in the Portuguese chronicle.

The first example can be found in the initial pages of the Chronicle, with the episode of Hercules' stay in the Iberian Peninsula. Once again, the Alfonsine basis is expanded, and the narrative acquires a more literary turn. Some characteristics of this hero of Antiquity, already existent in the 'royal version' (his goodwill towards his men, his role as defender of the humble, liberator of the good, etc.),[29] are now amplified (mainly in 1344b, chapter 7). Hercules is portrayed as an ideal leader who listens to his men, and who teaches and civilizes his peoples. Direct speech is used, making the narrative more lively and exciting, and some details remind us of an adventure novel. For instance, the duel between Hercules and Gerion is preceded by an exchange of rhetorically far-fetched, defiant and menacing letters between the two opponents. In the face of danger, Hercules' companions (the astrologer Allas and his nephew Espan) prove their loyalty, and while overestimating the power of Gerion, they cause a tragic pathos.[30] However, the passage that is more consistent with chivalric romances is the one where Hercules is depicted as a wandering knight who travels the world looking for new adventures:

> E, despois que ouve feytas todallas obras que em Espanha quis fazer, tornousse pera hyr em Grecia ou em outras partes honde achasse algūus

---

[29] The *General estoria* also includes the story of Hercules — Alfonso X el Sabio (general coord. by Pedro Sánchez-Prieto Borja), *General Estoria* (Madrid: Fundación José Antonio de Castro, 2009) — Part II (ed. by Belén Almeida). In accordance with the scope of this work, the story of Hercules is presented in its whole, which includes the adventures of the hero in the Iberian Peninsula, but these episodes are not over-considered, quite the opposite, since they are told in a far more succinct way than in the *Estoria de Espanna*. Some passages are already in line with a more literary penchant and with the chivalric spirit, such as in chap. 13 where it is said that everyone that looked at Hercules would be frozen out of respect for and fear of him (which is also said about the Cid) and that 'E Hércules era ya d'ante que allí viniesse muy nombrado por todas las tierras por sos fechos grandes e maravillosos que fazié' (Part II, vol. I, p. 40 — chap. 13) and latter on: 'e yéndose Ércules de Troya para Grecia salieron a él los omnes buenos e las otras gentes de aquellas tierras como a aquel que fuese su defendedor e que quebrantava las sobervias e vedava los tuertos,' (Part II, vol. II, p. 64 — chap. 405). This is also true for the 'royal version' of the *Estoria de Espanna*. But these works do not include the examples considered here, and the predominance of a novelesque tone is quite notorious in the second version of the *Crónica de 1344*. For a comparison between the story of Hercules as told by Rodrigo Jimenez de Rada, Alfonso X (*Estoria de Espanna*) and the second version of the *Crónica de 1344* see: Isabel de Barros Dias, 'Le Duel des géants' in Rosanna Brusegan, Alessandro Zironi, Anne Berthelot and Danielle Buschinger (eds.), *L'Antichitá nella Cultura Europea del Medioevo: L'Antiquité dans la Culture Européenne du Moyen Age* (Greifswald: Reineke-Verlag, 1998), pp. 195–205.

[30] 'nos nõ partimos contigo de Grecia por estar esguardando as batalhas que tu fezesses mas por nos avermos parte dos teus grandes feytos e morrermos e vyvermos ante ti; ca se os deusses por nossos pecados e aventuyra nos fossem ẽ contrairo e tu morresses ẽno campo sen nos, esto nos seerya grande confuson; ca muyto melhor he a nos morrer ante ty que tu ante nos, ca tu podes cobrar muytos e bõos cavalleyros melhores que nos e nos nũca podemos cobrar tal senhor e amigo come ty,' (1344b, vol. II, p. 24 — chap. 7).

feytos grandes e perigosos pera lhe dar acabamento, como aquelle que era o mais esforçado e mais valente e mais ligeyro que entom no mundo avya. (1344b, vol. II: p. 30 — chap. 9)

[After he had accomplished all the feats that he had set out to do in Spain, he headed for Greece or to any other place where he could accomplish some great and dangerous deeds, as he was the most diligent, brave and swift (man) in the world at that time.]

This writing style, similar to that of chivalric romances, is patent at various points of the narrative, often amplifying the text of the 'royal version' of the *Estoria de Espanna*. This occurs for instance in the description of the character of King Teuderigo,[31] in a passage that also emphasizes the characteristics of the 'good king', a *topos* already addressed above. Another example is the courtly answer of the future King Bamba when he was still a farmer.[32] Other examples of this trend can be found in certain passages about battles,[33] and include a description of the beauty of an army, reminiscent of the *sirventès* by Bertrand de Born.[34]

Still another passage where romance influence can be seen is in the account

---

[31] 'ē este āno, ouvyndo dizer Theuderigo, rey dos Estrogodos, como Guysalaito, rey dos Godos, era desterrado por sua grāde covardice e a terra estava sem senhor, e veendo outrossy como o reyno e terras dos Godos perteencia a seu neto Amallarico, porende, avydo conselho, ajuntou sua hoste muy grande e foisse pera as Espanhas e tornou logo a terra a seu senhoryo. // E esto foy por duas cousas: a primeira, por que elle era muy nobre rey em condiçoões e esforçado ē cavallarya e muy recebedor dos boos e faagueyro e de boo doayro a todos e justiçoso em todo tempo e logar; a segunda, por que elle nō demandava o reyno / pera sy mas pera seu neto Amallarico que era godo.' (1344b, vol. II, p. 165 — chap 106). At this point the *Estoria de Espanna* states: 'cuenta la estoria que quando el rey Theoderigo oyo dezir de como fuxiera el rey Gisalaygo et la tierra estaua sin sennor, que se uino pora las Espannas. E los godos por que uiron que su sennor Amalarigo era ninno, et que non auie edad pora mantener el regno dieronle el regno quel gouernasse yl mantouiesse en logar de su nieto Amalarigo.' (PCG, vol. I, p. 249a — chap. 440). The passage does not occur in 1344a.

[32] '— Amigos, se vos sodes homeēs humanoaes e nō fantasmas, ben devedes entender que as grandes cavallarias e grandes façanhas que a muy nobre gente dos Godos sempre fezeron, nom foy com taaes reis como eu.' (1344b, II: 232 -chap. 156). This answer does not occur in the *Estoria de Espanna* (cf. PCG, chap. 513), nor in the first version of the *Crónica de 1344* (cf. 1344a — chap. 73).

[33] For instance 'Mas el rey Theoderedo, a que nō era escaecido os grandes feytos d'armas e a grande nobreza dos Godos, andava muy esforçado na batalha, matando e feryndo seus ēmiigos e esforçādo a nobre companha dos Godos que fezesse bem' (1344b, II: 141 — chap 87) whereas *Estoria de Espanna* states 'Estonces Theuderedo, rey de los godos, andaua a todas partes por la su huest, esforçando los suyos et auiuando los que lidiassen,' (PCG, vol. I, p. 235b — chap. 413). The passage does not occur in 1344a.

[34] 'Depois que el rey deu este mandado, moveron as aazes pera a villa per tal ordenança que hūu nom trassaya pello outro em nē hūa cousa. Mas, quem poderia contar a grāde fremosura daquelas aazes assi ordenadas? Ca en meo dellas hyam as bandeiras del rey nobremente acompanhadas; e desi as dos capitaāes, cada hūa ē seu logar. O sōo das trombetas e reluzir das armas, esto era de maravylhar que, do resprendor que dellas saya cō o ferir do sol que em ellas dava, quē poderia esto dereytamente esguardar?' (1344b, II: 252 — chap. 164). The same passage in *Estoria de Espanna* is far less emotive: 'E en uiniendo el con toda su hueste, daua el sol que se leuantaua estonces en las armas, et el color de las armas resplandescie sobre la tierra; e tan fremosamientre yuan todos et tan bien parescien que non a cosa que tan bien pudiesse semeiar, e tan bien yuan ordenados et tan apuestamientre que ninguno non salie dell az, mas cada uno tenie muy bien so logar;' (PCG, I: 291b — chap. 522). The passage is absent from 1344a (cf. 1344a — chap. 73).

of the legend of Alfonso X's blasphemy, in which a reference to the prophecies of a Greek woman are evocative of the plots of Byzantine novels. Later on in the text Queen Beatrice sighs and cries as a consequence of her thoughts, and King Ferdinand asks her to explain the reason for such grief.[35] This is quite similar to a passage in the novel *Erec et Enide*, by Chrétien de Troyes, where Enide's tear-shedding drives Erec to his chivalric adventures.

These passages probably give us some hints about the readings and literary tastes of the redactor of the second version of the *Chronicle of 1344*. In fact, the books that an author reads usually influence his way of writing, especially in the *topoi* he chooses and in the way he composes his own narratives. Chivalric romances and characters were known in the Iberian Peninsula from the thirteenth century onwards.[36] Chivalric models are known to have been seen as ideals for historical figures.[37] It is therefore not surprising that our author was familiar with some of these romances and enjoyed their style, to the extent that he used them as a model for his own writing. In fact, a person's idiosyncratic universe, composed of ideas, beliefs, ideals and readings, is bound to show up

---

[35] 'E hũu dia aconteceo que elrey / dom Fernando e a raynha sua molher, depois que se levantaron de dormir a sesta, demandou el rey vinho e fruita ẽ sua camara. E o iffante dom Afonso tomou a copa e servyo a seu padre e a sua madre, dandolhes o vinho muy apostamente. E a raynha pos os olhos en el, esguardandoo con grande femença, e deu hũu grande sospiro e começou de chorar. E el rey, quando tal sospiro vyo, nõ o teve en pouco. E, depois que o iffante e todollos outros foron fora da camara, preguntou el rey aa rainha por que dera aquelle sospiro quando vira seu filho o iffante servir de copa:' (1344b, IV: 379).

[36] There are references to Arthurian heroes, especially regarding early Galician-Portuguese lyric poetry. For further information on this matter, see the classical book by William J. Entwistle, *The Arthurian Legend in the Literatures of the Spanish Peninsula* (London and Toronto: J. M. Dent & Sons Ltd; New York: E. P. Dutton & Co., 1925). See also the more specific article by Harvey L. Sharrer, 'La materia de Bretaña en la poesía Gallego-Portuguesa', in *Actas del I Congreso de la Asociación Hispánica de Literatura Medieval*, ed. by Vicente Beltrán (Barcelona: Promociones y Publicaciones Universitarias, 1988), pp. 561–69. Also fundamental to this matter is the article by Ivo Castro, 'Sobre a data da introdução na Península Ibérica do ciclo arturiano da Post-Vulgata', *Boletim de Filologia*, 28 (1983), 81–98.

[37] As underlined by António José Saraiva, *O crepúsculo da Idade Média em Portugal* (Lisbon: Gradiva, 1998): 'A *Crónica do Condestabre de Portugal*, aparecida em manuscrito em 1433 e impressa em 1526, diz que o jovem Nun'Álvares "usava muito de ouvir e ler livros de histórias, especialmente usava mais ler a estoria de Galaaz em que se continha a soma da Távola Redonda" (cap. IV). E Fernão Lopes conta, na *Crónica de D. João I*, que os guerreiros de D. João I, gracejando, se comparavam a Galaaz, a Tristão, a Lançarote e a outros companheiros da Távola Redonda, dizendo que só faltava ali o bom rei Artur (2ª parte, cap.76)' (p. 72); and some pages before: 'Segundo a *Crónica do Condestabre*, Nun'Álvares "usava muito de ouvir e ler livros de estórias; especialmente usava mais ler a estória de Galaaz em que se continha a suma da Távola Redonda; e porque em ela achava que, por virtude de virgindade que em ele houve e em que perseverou, Galaaz acabara grandes e notáveis feitos que outros não puderam acabar. E ele desejava muito de o parecer em alguma guisa, e muitas vezes em si cuidava de ser virgem, se a Deus prouvesse. E por isto ele era mui afastado do que lhe seu pai falara em jeito de casamento"' (p. 57). For earlier times and from an historical point of view see also José Mattoso, *Ricos-homens, infanções e cavaleiros* (Lisbon: Guimarães Editores, 1998), who studies the relationship among literary models (mainly epic) and the formation of an heroic aura as part of some noble families' strategies for power, and Luís Krus, *A concepção nobiliárquica no espaço ibérico, 1280–1380* (Lisbon: FCG / JNICT, 1994) who addresses the question of the preservation of the ideals and values of the nobility as a way to justify their class in times of decadence and the role that chivalry literature played in this context. After all, novels kept alive ideals like the ones of Crusades, Reconquest and Chivalry long after their decline...

when this person is composing a text. The same happens when new features occur or are underlined in a specific version of a work, and that can give us some hints on the profile of its author.

Conclusion

The above mentioned trends are very comprehensive and do not reveal any specific author for the second version of the *Chronicle of 1344*, but we believe that it contributes to the definition of a specific profile. This person probably had strong convictions about the role of the Church in the world,[38] and was familiar with 'mirrors for princes' and court literature.[39] He could have been a reader, or a translator — or even a writer — of this kind of literature. He was certainly a cultivated person.

This article is only the first step in a long process. It is important to take a deeper look, and discuss the specific characteristics of the second version of the *Chronicle of 1344*. We hope that the evidence brought forward, and the reflections developed in this article will be an initial step towards further research and, hopefully, a stimulus for new hypothesis and discoveries.

---

[38] The clerical trend obviously does not require that the author of the second version of the *Chronicle of 1344* be a friar; he could have been so, but he could have also been a layman who sympathized with the options of the 'Observantes'. It is well known that Franciscanism had wide acceptance among laymen, including many noble families. In fact, Mendicants (and Franciscans) have been teachers, chaplains, confessors and counsellors to many aristocratic families who often made large donations to Mendicant convents and chose them as burial site. Also, the libraries of nobles commonly had devotional books by mendicant authors. On the influence of the Mendicant orders in secular devotion, see José Mattoso, *Identificação de um país: ensaio sobre as origens de Portugal, 1096-1325 — I — Oposição* (Lisbon: Estampa, 1995), pp. 421-22, Isabel Beceiro Pita, 'De las peregrinaciones al viaje interior: las transformaciones en la religiosidad nobiliar castellana' *Cahiers d'Études Hispaniques Médiévales*, 30 (2007), 109-25 (specifically on mendicant spirituality and ideal models, see p. 116) and Isabel Beceiro Pita, 'La nobleza y las órdenes mendicantes en Castilla (1350-1530)', in *idem* (dir.), *Poder, piedad y devoción: Castilla y su entorno. Siglos XII-XV* (Madrid: Sílex: 2014) pp. 319-58.

[39] This trend does not require this author to be a layman. Ramon Llull, for instance, was a Franciscan friar who also wrote literary works and composed a book on the order of chivalry. The influence of this Franciscan in the Portuguese culture of the end of the fourteenth century is underlined by Francisco da Gama Caeiro, 'A cultura portuguesa no último quartel do século XIV' (pp. 376-77). Besides, the closeness between mendicants and noblemen favoured the incorporation of religious motives in chivalrous models. Admission to Mendicant monasteries was often chosen as an option for the second sons of the aristocratic families, as well as for the retreat of nobles at the end of their lives or when they decided to abandon worldly wealth (some took clerical orders, but others didn't). Nuno Álvares Pereira (already mentioned in note 37) is a good example of this, since he was a layman and a warrior, appreciated chivalric romances and in the last period of his life joined a convent. On this matters, see the articles in Isabel Beceiro Pita (dir.), *Poder, Piedad y Devoción. Castilla y su entorno. Siglos XII-XV* (Madrid: Sílex: 2014) by Isabel Beceiro Pita, 'La nobleza y las órdenes mendicantes en Castilla (1350-1530)', pp. 319-58 and by Maria de Lurdes Rosa, 'Exercício do poder e salvação da alma: a *fuga mundi* nos círculos cortesãos tardo-medievais portugueses', pp. 423-51 (on noblemen that have abandoned their place in society and entered monasteries, often in the position of 'Observantes', and on cases of 'private asceticism' of persons that lived in the court).

The Subversion of Hate Literature in Anrique da Mota's *Farce of the Tailor*

ANNA MATHESON

Université Rennes 2

In his *Farce of the Tailor*, written sometime between 1497 and 1506, Anrique da Mota uses a number of anti-Semitic stereotypes so that the farce, at first glance, appears to be an overt satire deriding New Christians.[1] However, as this paper will show, there is in fact an underlying dialogue to the text: Mota takes these very same anti-Semitic stereotypes and subtly turns them on their heads to create a hidden, parallel reading. In so doing, his farce is actually a very serious polemic on the topic of conversion and, more specifically, apostasy. Mota makes it clear that converts have no rights or place in early sixteenth-century Portuguese society, but there is a sympathetic strain to his argument: in what is actually a sensitive depiction of the *converso*'s state of alienation and plight for social justice, Mota is making a statement against the practice of coerced conversion rather than attacking *conversos* themselves.

Previous scholars who have noted a sympathetic quality to Mota's message include José Leite de Vasconcellos, Andrée Crabbé Rocha, and Neil T. Miller, yet these discussions have, due to restrictions of space and scope, only been cursory; a detailed study of Mota's literary artistry in conveying this message has not yet been accomplished.[2] The present article therefore builds on their discussions by means of close textual analysis that will highlight the above-mentioned use of stereotypes and shed light on how they are manipulated. Most importantly, it will reveal the magnitude of Mota's social commentary which, as I shall argue, may be informed by popular notions of Jewish rabbinical tradition and which, as will be seen, has been misrepresented in its most recent study by Reuven Faingold in 1991.[3] The discussion will also further our knowledge

---

[1] Editions of this farce are found in *Farsa do Alfaiate: Uma das Mais Antigas Peças do Teatro Português*, ed. by José Leite de Vasconcellos (Lisbon: Edições Lusitania, 1924); *Cancioneiro Geral de Garcia de Resende*, ed. by Andrée Crabbé Rocha, vol. v (Lisbon: Centro do Livro Brasileiro, 1973), pp. 202–11; Neil T. Miller, *Obras de Henrique da Mota: As Origens do Teatro Ibérico* (Lisbon: Livraria Sá da Costa, 1982), pp. 402–11; Aida Fernandes Dias, *Cancioneiro Geral de Garcia de Resende*, vol. IV (Lisbon: Imprensa Nacional–Casa da Moeda, 1993), pp. 168–76; and *Obras de Anrique da Mota*, ed. by Osório Mateus et al. (Lisbon: Comissão Nacional para as Comemorações dos Descobrimentos Portugueses, 1999), pp. 51–58. I will be citing from Vasconcellos's authoritative study and edition. All translations are mine unless otherwise noted.
[2] Vasconcellos, *Farsa*, pp. 47–49; Andrée Crabbé Rocha, *Esboços Dramáticos no Cancioneiro Geral* (Coimbra: Coimbra Editora, 1951), p. 37; and Miller, *Obras*, p. 252.
[3] Reuven Faingold, 'Judíos y conversos en el teatro portugués pre-vicentino: la *Farsa do alfaiate* en el

of Mota's biography by quietly correcting certain historical inaccuracies in previous discussions of archival documents concerning Mota and his family.[4]

Henrique da Mota: Life and Times

Little is known about our author's birth and death. Though it is suspected that Mota was born in the late third or early final quarter of the fifteenth century, our only evidence for Mota's dates is the chronological range of the documents either ascribed to him or in which he is mentioned. As Miller has shown, these date from 1499 to 1545.[5]

Mota was himself an Old Christian and a lay magistrate: he was a *juiz dos órfãos* [judge of orphans] in and around Óbidos, north of Lisbon. In his capacity as judge of orphans, he would have presided over all civil cases involving orphans under the age of twenty-five, as well as the destitute (*prodiguos*) and persons of unsound mind.[6] Yet it is significant that, prior to the forced conversions of 1497, the judge of orphans would sometimes also have heard civil and criminal cases between Christians and Jews or Muslims, where the Jew or the Muslim was the plaintiff.[7] Unfortunately, we do not know whether Mota ever served in this capacity of magistrate for Muslims and Jews, nor do we know whether he took up the position of judge of orphans prior to 1497; no judicial records from his term have yet come to light. Anselmo Braamcamp Freire suspects that Mota was appointed to the position by Queen Leonor, who acquired jurisdiction of the region in 1482, since the 'relatively complete' *Chancelaria de D. Manuel* does not include his notice of hire.[8] In fact, Manuel's registry is hardly complete and many documents from his chancery are now barely legible.[9] Knowing, as we do, that D. Leonor was our poet Mota's patron, she may well have secured a position for her protégé, although the date when he was appointed or elected to the office

---

Cancioneiro geral de Garcia de Resende', *Sefarad*, 51.1 (1991), 23–50. See below, note 28.

[4] A full account of the argument summarized here will appear in a separate monograph containing an English translation of the play: Anna Matheson, *The Polemics of Conversion: The Representation of the Apostate in Anrique da Mota's 'Farce of the Tailor'* (in preparation).

[5] Miller, *Obras*, pp. 123–52.

[6] Full details on the responsibilities of the *juiz dos órfãos* are found in book 1, title 67 of the *Ordenações Manuelinas* (henceforth *OM*), promulgated in 1512. A glimpse of his role in the earlier Afonsine Code is found in *Ordenações Afonsinas* (*OA*) I. 26. 33–39; II. 92; IV. 82–93 and 112. Some documented instances of judges 'of orphans, Jews, and Muslims' are collected in Henrique da Gama Barros, 'Judeus e Mouros em Portugal em Tempos Passados', *Revista Lusitana*, 34 (1936), 165–265 and 35 (1937), 161–238 (docs. 14, 145, 146, and 147).

[7] Lisbon, Arquivo Nacional da Torre do Tombo (ANTT), Leitura Nova, *Livro 4 de Odiana*, fols 85^v–86^v; ANTT, *Chancelaria de D. João II*, book 6, fol. 88^{r-v}; and book 21, fol. 101^r. These documents are discussed in Maria José Pimenta Ferro Tavares, *Os Judeus em Portugal no Século XV*, vol. I (Lisbon: Universidade Nova de Lisboa, Faculdade de Ciências Sociais e Humanas, 1982), p. 118 note 70.

[8] Anselmo Braamcamp Freire, *Vida e Obras de Gil Vicente: Trovador, Mestre da Balança* (Lisbon: Edição da Revista Ocidente, 1944), p. 64.

[9] Fernando Portugal, 'A Chancelaria de D. Manuel', *Ethnos*, 6 (1969), 3–12; Pedro A. de Azevedo and António Baião, *O Arquivo da Torre do Tombo: Sua História, Corpos que o Compõem e Organização* (Lisbon: Livros Horizonte, 1989), pp. 32–33.

cannot be confirmed.[10] The earliest surviving reference to Mota employed as a judge of orphans is in a literary text that dates to *c.* 1509: he appears as a character in his own lyrical piece known as *O Processo de Vasco Abul* [The Lawsuit of Vasco Abul], where he is a judge of orphans who is presented with an outlandish legal quandary involving an old lecher and a young, orphaned belly dancer.[11] Later evidence corroborating Mota's employment as a judge of orphans in the Óbidos region is, according to Freire, to be found in a certificate that is attached to a royal mandate dated 15 May 1521, but which subsequent scholars have not been able to locate and verify.[12]

Also significant for our purposes, Mota was a member of D. Manuel's court in the years following the edict of expulsion of 1496: a letter dated 1499 stipulates that he was commissioned with the delivery of a royal message to the *fidalgo* Anrique da Silveira, and it reveals that Mota was an *escudeiro del rei* (the lowest grade within the Portuguese ranks of nobility) who lived in Bombarral (a village close to Óbidos).[13] After the edict was promulgated, D. Manuel is known to have resorted to a number of coercive measures in order to encourage the Jews to convert and remain in Portugal. These tactics included a decree, published 15 December 1496, stating that Jews who converted to Christianity could stay in Portugal and buy back their property for the same price at which it was sold.[14] Writs were sent to the town council of Porto (31 December 1496) and the port of Buarcos (2 January 1497) stating that Jews were not to leave the country without a special royal licence — any fugitive Jews or ship's captains who assisted them in leaving would lose their property.[15] Children under the age of fourteen were removed from their Jewish parents, baptized, and adopted into Catholic families, to be given back to their parents only if they themselves converted. Parents obstinate in their faith were furthermore faced with financial duress, since the baptized children were to be paid two-thirds of their

---

[10] Mário de Sampayo Ribeiro, 'A Rainha Dona Leonor de Lancastre e os Alvores do Teatro Português', *Ocidente*, 56 (1959), 69–82 (pp. 72–79); and Ivo Carneiro de Sousa, *A Rainha D. Leonor (1458–1525): Poder, Misericórdia, Religiosidade e Espiritualidade no Portugal do Renascimento* (Lisbon: Fundação Calouste Gulbenkian, 2002), pp. 858–59. On the powers exercised by D. Leonor as a dowager, see *OA* II. 40 and the later *OM* II. 26.
[11] The date of this text is discussed by Alina Villalva, *Vasco Abul* (Lisbon: Quimera, 1989; e-book, 2005); Miller, *Obras*, pp. 145–46; Freire, *Vida e Obras*, pp. 62–64.
[12] Freire, *Vida e Obras*, p. 63. Freire references Gaspar Alvares de Lousada Machado's *Sumarios de Todas as Doações e Chancelarias da Torre do Tombo*, vol. III, fol. 274^v, which I have not been able to locate and consult despite the kind efforts of the staff at ANTT and the Biblioteca Nacional de Portugal.
[13] ANTT, *Chancelaria de D. Manuel I*, book 16, fols 135^v–36^r; transcribed by Miller in *Obras*, pp. 457–59.
[14] Manuel Pedro Serra and Luís Miguel Duarte, *Actas de Vereação de Loulé, Século XV*, separata de *Revista al'-Ulyā*, 10 (Loulé, 2004), pp. 227–29 (*non vidi*).
[15] Artur de Magalhães Basto, *Livro Antigo de Cartas e Provisões dos Senhores Reis D. Afonso V, D. João II e D. Manuel I do Arquivo Municipal do Porto* (Porto: Câmara Municipal do Porto, 1940), pp. 107–08 doc. 69; Abílio José Salgado and Anastásia Salgado Mestrinho, *Registos dos Reinados de D. João II e de D. Manuel I* (Lisbon: Ministério da Saúde, 1996), p. 377.

inheritance immediately upon their conversion.[16] The final outcome was that in 1497 those Jews who had resisted these coercive measures, having chosen to retain their religious integrity and who wished to leave the country now were for the most part either martyred or forcibly converted to Christianity. These actions, the king maintained, were carried out in accordance with what the Franciscan theologian John Duns Scotus had described as the Christian ruler's right and duty to forcibly convert Jews.[17]

This was a time of great social upheaval, and many tried to flee even after the ordeals of 1497. In 1499, the same year in which the aforementioned document describing Mota as an *escudeiro* of the king was written, D. Manuel issued a decree that prohibited New Christians (that is, all those converted in 1497) from exiting the country.[18] One can surmise from all this that, as an *escudeiro da casa del Rei*, our author would have had something of an insider's perspective on court affairs in the turbulent years that followed the forced conversions.

In fact, Mota came from a line of Portuguese courtiers. His father, Gonçalo da Mota, was an *escudeiro criado* of Afonso V and João II. As such, he would have been schooled and raised in the Portuguese court alongside the *infantes*.[19] His grandfather, João da Mota, was also an *escudeiro*, and he was granted land comprising vineyards and orchards in Bombarral, in which property the kings themselves would stay when travelling through the area.[20] In 1509, Anrique da Mota was elevated from the status of *escudeiro* to *cavaleiro fidalgo* and he received his own coat of arms.[21] On 12 August 1527, after the death of his patron, the dowager Queen Leonor, in 1525, an Anrique da Mota — who is believed to be the same individual as our author — was appointed to the position of *escrivão*

---

[16] François Soyer enumerates and discusses these and other pressure tactics used by D. Manuel in *The Persecution of the Jews and Muslims of Portugal: King Manuel I and the End of Religious Tolerance (1496-7)* (Leiden: Brill, 2007), pp. 193-218. See also Giuseppe Marcocci, '"... per capillos adductos ad pillam": Il dibattito cinquecentesco sulla validità del battesimo forzato degli ebrei in Portogallo (1496-1497)', in *Salvezza delle anime disciplina dei corpi*, ed. by Adriano Prosperi (Pisa: Edizioni della Normale, 2006), pp. 339-423 (pp. 355-67).

[17] Arguments presented by D. Manuel in defence of the forced conversion are summarized, along with the most popular arguments both for and against the juridical and theological validity of forced baptism, in Marcocci, 'per capillos' pp. 345-50 and 363-81.

[18] This decree is preserved in *OM* V. 82.

[19] Letter issued by João III in Évora, 15 November 1533, in ANTT, *Chancelaria de D. João III*, book 46, fols 90^v-91^r; transcribed in Neil T. Miller, 'Henrique da Mota and the Origins of Iberian Drama' (unpublished doctoral thesis, City University New York, 1972), p. 507. Gonçalo da Mota is also described as an *escudeiro criado* (and a resident of Bombarral) in a letter of privilege written by João II in 1486 in ANTT, *Chancelaria de D. João II*, book 8, fol. 55^r and in other letters by the same king dated 23 July and 27 August 1487 (*Chancelaria de D. João II*, book 20, fols 129^{r-v} and 188^{r-v}; transcribed by Miller, 'Henrique', pp. 509-12). For details on the *escudeiro criado* in the fifteenth century, see Rita Costa Gomes, *The Making of a Court Society: Kings and Nobles in Late Medieval Portugal*, trans. by A. Aiken (Cambridge: Cambridge University Press, 2003), pp. 231-41.

[20] ANTT, *Chancelaria de D. João III*, book 46, fols 90^v-91^r (transcribed in Miller, 'Henrique', p. 507); ANTT, Carta de Armas de Anrique da Mota, dated 18 July 1509 (in Cartas de armas, caixa 1, n.º 1; transcribed in Mateus, *Obras*, pp. 21-22).

[21] ANTT, Carta de Armas de Anrique da Mota.

da câmara real [royal clerk] to João III.²² No doubt, Mota was upwardly social, yet his longstanding role of guardian of the poor as judge of orphans may help to explain the sensitivity expressed in his lyrical social commentaries.²³

The Farce of the Tailor: Summary and Date

Anrique da Mota's lyrical works are preserved in folios 201^v–11^r of the *Cancioneiro Geral*, an anthology of court literature — mainly poetry and dramatic works composed during the years 1450 to 1516 — that was compiled by the chronicler and poet Garcia de Resende, dedicated to D. Manuel's fourteen-year-old son, Prince João (later João III), and printed in 1516.²⁴

Mota's works include five pieces of early performance art that Miller refers to as dramatic dialogues.²⁵ In most of these dialogues, Mota uses the common dramatic form of the mock trial; the present study is focused on one such mock trial, the one popularly known as *A Farsa do Alfaiate* [The Farce of the Tailor].²⁶ This comedic piece, which is only 260 lines long, opens with the protagonist, a *converso* tailor named Manuel, lamenting the loss of a gold coin he had been saving. He cannot determine whether it was mislaid or stolen, but he blames the unfortunate loss on the fact that he was baptized, as no good has come to him since. He is in a state of utter despair and, just as he resolves to take the matter to his lord, D. Diogo, D. João enters the scene. This Lord D. Diogo is believed to be the historical D. Diogo de Noronha, son of D. Pedro de Meneses, the Marquis of Vila-Real, and D. João is believed to be D. Diogo's brother, D. João de Noronha, grand prior of Santa Cruz Monastery in Coimbra.²⁷ The

---

²² His letter of appointment is preserved in ANTT, *Chancelaria de D. João III*, book 30, fol. 131^v; transcribed in Miller, *Obras*, p. 505.
²³ For full details on Mota's life and works, see Miller, *Obras*; and Mateus, *Obras*.
²⁴ Garcia de Resende (ed.), *Cancioneiro Geral* (Lisbon: Herman de Campos, 1516).
²⁵ For discussion of the theatrical merit of these pieces, including arguments that they transcend the common *entremês* (which would have been recited by one, single reader responsible for the voices of all *dramatis personae*) and instead bear the traits of stage theatre, predating the plays of Gil Vicente, see Vasconcellos, *Farsa*; Gustavo de Matos Sequeira, 'A Farsa do Alfaiate', *Teatro de Outros Tempos* (Lisbon: [n. pub.], 1933), pp. 9–16 (p. 15); Rocha, *Esboços Dramáticos*, p. 10; Ribeiro, 'Rainha Dona Leonor', p. 73; Luciana Stegagno Picchio, 'Osservazioni sull'uso di alcuni termini nell'antico teatro portoghese', *Boletim de Filologia*, 19 (1960), 131–43.
²⁶ The rubric in the *Cancioneiro Geral* introduces this piece as 'D'Anrique da Mota a um Alfaiate de dom Diogo sobre um cruzado que lhe furtaram no Bombarral' (Mateus, *Obras*, p. 51); '[Lyrics] by Anrique da Mota to a tailor of D. Diogo's regarding a coin that was stolen from him in Bombarral'.
²⁷ Vasconcellos, *Farsa*, pp. 35 and 38–39; Miller, *Obras*, pp. 142–43. Dom Diogo features in another of Mota's dialogues, the one popularly known as *A Lamentaçao da Mula* [The Mule's Lament]. Dom João de Noronha is ridiculed in a satirical poem by Mota that was censored for its critique of corruption within the Church and that bears the heading 'D'Anrique da Mota a dom João de Noronha e a dom Sancho seu irmão porque se foram confessar a sam Bernaldim na metade de verão, levando consig o vigairo D'Óvidos que é muito gordo, e vieram jantar a um lugar que chamam Os Giraldos e nom acharam vinho pera beber' [[Lyrics] by Anrique da Mota to D. João de Noronha and his brother, D. Sancho, because they went to confess in São Bernardino in the middle of summer, bringing with them the vicar of Óbidos, who is very fat, and they went to dine at a place called Os Giraldos and they could not find wine to drink] (Mateus, *Obras*, pp. 42–44 and 63–79). Dom Diogo was *comendador mór* of

grand prior directs the *converso* to the chapel of the Holy Spirit instead, saying that he should present himself as a penitent supplicant so that he may learn through divine intervention who has taken his coin. Manuel goes to the chapel and offers an awkward prayer for assistance. He grows frustrated at the lack of an immediate response from the Holy Spirit and leaves the sanctuary in a huff. He then encounters a rustic, João de Belas, along the road. The rustic tells him, in a vague and roundabout way, of some news he has learnt about an item that was found. Despite the rustic's comically vague story, Manuel leaps to the conclusion that the item found is his *cruzado*. He thanks the rustic for having identified the man who found his coin, and he runs to the judge with the news. The judge agrees to assist Manuel in recuperating his *cruzado*, needing only the name of the culprit to recover the coin. However, the *converso* cannot name the culprit; instead, he gives an ambiguous description of him based on the story he heard earlier from the rustic buffoon, João de Belas. The farce then ends with the judge, having grown impatient with the tailor's ramblings and lack of clear evidence, ruling that the lost coin had been stolen by Manuel in the first place, since he acquired it without proper fear of God.

While the precise date at which this text was composed has not been confirmed, internal evidence points to the period between 1497 and 1506. Our protagonist describes himself as a voluntary convert:

> Çerto eu naçy maa ora,
> em pior fuy bautizado,
> pois desemtam atègora
> sempre em mym mofina mora,
> [...]
> tudo he bem empreguado
> em mim, pois tomey de grado
> esta ley noua de graça. (ll. 41–50)
>
> [For certain I was born at a bad hour,
> at an even worse hour I was baptized,
> since from that time until now
> misery always resides in me,
> [...]
> all is well deserved
> in me, since I willingly accepted
> this new law of Christ.]

Many believe that the mention of the 'new law of Christ' in the last line of this passage is a reference to the nationwide forced conversion of the Jews in 1497,

---

the Ordem de Cristo, *alcaide mór* of Óbidos, and *senhor dos direitos* of Salir do Porto. His second wife was D. Filipa de Ataíde, granddaughter of Nuno Vaz de Castelo-Branco, Lord of Bombarral, according to one of the two traditions preserved in António Caetano de Sousa's *Provas da História Genealógica da Casa Real Portuguesa*, vol. IX (Lisbon: Lisboa Occidental: Na officina Sylviana da Academia Real, 1742), p. 64. She was Nuno's great-granddaughter in the alternative tradition in vol. v (Lisbon: Lisboa Occidental: Na officina Sylviana da Academia Real 1738), p. 196.

and they therefore hold that the text could not have been written before this date.[28] Whether or not they are correct in their reading of this line, there is no doubt that Manuel expresses regret that his conversion had been voluntary and that he had not put up any resistance. This is exemplified, for example, in his exclamation, 'Oxalá fôra batalha!' [If only there had been a fight!] (l. 88). I will be arguing that, by having the *converso* lament his voluntary conversion, our author is presenting his protagonist as a repentant *meshumad*, a common term in twelfth- to fifteenth-century Jewish *responsa* literature, in which a distinction was often made between forced converts (*anusim*) and voluntary converts (*meshumadim*).[29] We will be returning to this point below, but it is important to signal now that the distinction between forced and voluntary converts would have had special relevance in Portugal after the forced conversions. The Jewish community would no doubt have distinguished between those who were forcibly baptized and those who had converted willingly when under social and economic pressure, in 1496, and this may support the argument that 1497 is the earliest possible date when the farce could have been composed. The *terminus ad quem* is 1506 since this is the year that one of the characters, Grand Prior D. João de Noronha, died, and the representation of a character in a dialogue *post mortem* would have been unlikely.[30]

Condemnation of the Convert

The Farce of the Tailor is rather telling about what a man of law has to say about the rights of converts: in short, they have no rights. This is made clear in Manuel's despair upon the loss of his coin, since he does not know where to turn to obtain justice. He fears that the Old Christian judge will not defend his rights:

> Eu nam ssey que mal eu fiz,
> que tal perda me conuenha!
> O coraçam quá me diz
> que vá buscar o juiz,
> & creo que bem me venha.
> E direy que me mantenha
> em justiça com ssa vara.
> Oo quem me dera ter grenha!
> pois nam tenho quem me tenha,
> eu por m'y m'arrepelara! (ll. 61–70)

---

[28] Vasconcellos, *Farsa*, p. 34; Luciana Stegagno Picchio, *Storia del teatro portoghese* (Rome: Edizioni dell'Ateneo, 1964), p. 91; Miller, *Obras*, pp. 142–44. These scholars give 1496 as the year of the *conversão geral*, however, it is well known that the forced conversions occurred in 1497 (Soyer, *Persecution*, pp. 218–31). Reuven Faingold also regards this piece as having been written after the forced conversions of 1497, but his analysis of the farce, based on his interpretation of Manuel as a forced convert, is not supported in the text: 'Judíos y conversos', pp. 41–43.
[29] The statement above is an oversimplification: rabbinical ideas differed regarding what constitutes duress and 'forced' conversion, and the *anusim/meshumadim* dichotomy becomes somewhat skewed, if not abandoned in some of the discussions. This will be discussed below.
[30] Vasconcellos, *Farsa*, p. 35; Jorge de Sena, 'Anrique da Mota ou Inês em Prosa e Verso', *Ocidente*, 73 (1967), 604–18 (p. 605 note 223).

> [I don't know what wrong I did
> to deserve such a loss!
> The heart that beats within me says
> that I should go and fetch the judge,
> and I believe that good will come of it.
> I will ask him to maintain me
> in justice with his staff.
> Oh, would that I had wild, unruly hair!
> Since I have no one to defend me,
> I would pull it out myself!]

He resolves to go to his lord, D. Diogo, who has always shown him favour:

> Mas porem sse o Ssenhor
> Dom Dyogue ysto ssabe,
> segundo me tem amor,
> porque ssam sseu seruidor (ll. 76–79)

> [But, however, if Lord
> Dom Diogo were to know of this,
> *he* has much affection for me
> because I am his client]

This may or may not be a comment on the tight-knit relationship between some Jews and the Portuguese nobility.[31] There is certain irony in the fact that the first figure Manuel meets on his path for justice is a Christian religious figure, Grand Prior D. João; a religious figure from his ancestral faith, the *rabbi menor* (lower rabbi), would have been Manuel's first point of contact regarding any issues of faith or justice. Though Manuel first rejects the grand prior's assistance, the cleric succeeds in pushing him towards a Christian route for legal recourse (he sends him to pray in the chapel of the Holy Spirit). But this route is not satisfactory as he does not get an immediate response from the Holy Spirit, and Manuel's initial fears concerning his lack of support within the Old Christian judicial system are reaffirmed by the Old Christian judge's verdict which ends the farce:

> Mas porem, porqu'aleguays
> ssynays com que m'embaçastes,
> por esses mesmos ssinays
> eu julgo, que vós percais
> o cruzado que furtastes,
> por c'assy como o ganhastes
> sem temor de Deos nem medo,
> a bofee bem no lograstes:
> & nam ssey como o goardastes,
> que sse nam perdeo mais çedo (ll. 251–60)

---

[31] On such ties, see Maria José Ferro Tavares, *Os Judeus em Portugal no Século XIV*, 2nd edn (Lisbon: Guimarães, 2000), p. 66.

> [But still, because you allege
> the description with which you confuse me,
> by the same description
> I deem that you lost
> the *cruzado* that you stole,
> for, since you won it
> without dread nor fear of God,
> by good faith, you rightfully deserve to lose it:
> and I do not know how you kept it,
> without having lost it much sooner]

No doubt, the text ends with a clear note of condemnation from the Old Christian judge.

Pere Ferré has recently suggested that, in the lines 'Mas yr-m'ey por essa terra, | como homem ssem ventura' (ll. 11–12), Mota makes an allusion to Gonzalo de Montalbán's poem 'Morir vos queredes, padre', which reads, 'Yrme he por esas tierras | como una muger errada'.[32] The latter poem describes an exchange between Princess Urraca and her dying father, Fernando I, King of León and Castile: in her successful petition to secure an inheritance of land, she warns that she would otherwise be forced to wander as a wanton woman, offering herself to Muslims and Christians alike. Ferré argues that Mota intends a comic counterpoint between the aristocrat's complaints to her father over a lack of royal inheritance and the complaints of an *indigno judío* [contemptible Jew] over the loss of a 'miserable *cruzado*'. Yet an attempt to draw similarities between these two plotlines seems strained, and Ferré's reading may be further complicated by potential issues regarding the chronological order of the two works (Montalbán's *floruit* is unknown and the earliest printed edition of his text has not been dated more precisely than to the first half of the sixteenth century).[33] It would seem that any similarity in the above-cited couplets may be more easily attributed to common influence or perhaps even more simply to a commonplace trope. Nevertheless, Ferré has approached Mota's work on the literal level alone and thus describes it as an anti-Semitic piece that contains 'Mota's biting critique of the Jews'.[34] He is not alone; Faingold has also recently interpreted an anti-Semitic message in Mota's text.[35] But, even if a parody of D. Urraca's distress has indeed been woven into the farce, let us reconsider where the author's sympathies (if we can use the term) lie.

---

[32] Pere Ferré, 'Breves notas sobre el teatro de Anrique da Mota y Gil Vicente', in *Em Louvor da Linguagem: Homenagem a Maria Leonor Carvalhão Buescu*, ed. by Maria Leonor Machado de Sousa et al. (Lisbon: Edições Colibri, 2003), pp. 97–110 (pp. 103–04).

[33] Ramón Menéndez Pidal, 'Morir vos queredes, padre', *Estudios sobre el romancero*, Obras completas de R. Menéndez Pidal, 11 (Madrid: Espasa-Calpe, 1973), pp. 107–23 (pp. 107–08).

[34] 'La enorme trascendencia puesta en esta pérdida del "cruzado" y, a su vez, el camino que tendrá que hacer como "homem sem ventura" [...] son suficiente claros para que el auditorio entienda la irónica crítica de Mota a los judíos' (Ferré, 'Breves notas', p. 104).

[35] Faingold, 'Judíos y conversos', pp. 47–50.

Literal Reading (*Converso* Ridiculed)

There seem to be two possible readings of this text: a literal Christian reading in which the *converso* is ridiculed, and an allegorical reading that is sympathetic to the moral-theological dilemma faced by Jews who were forced to either convert to Catholicism or attempt to leave the country. To begin with the literal reading that mocks the *converso*, we see from his opening monologue that Manuel's speech is characterized by Jewish expressions like *goayas* and *guyzeraa*, and one could argue that his *pranto* [lament] is a farcical exaggeration of the very serious melancholic style that *converso* authors commonly used to express sentiments of grief over their social circumstances and the sempiternal exile of the Hebrew nation.[36]

> Goayas, que sam destroçado!
> ay, Adonay, que farey!
> poys que quys o meu pecado
> que perdy o meu cruzado
> que por maas noytes guanhey!
> Goay de mym, onde m'irey,
> que rreçeba algum conforto?
> se o calo, abafarey...
> jur'em Deu, nam calarey,
> porque nessora ssam morto!
> [...]
> Guyzeraa, que gram tristura! (ll. 1–16)
>
> [Woe, that I am destroyed!
> Oh, Adonai, what will I do!
> Because I willed my sin
> I have lost my *cruzado*
> which I earned after many hard nights!
> Woe is me, where will I go
> to find any consolation?
> If I remain silent, I will suffocate.
> By God, I will not remain silent,
> for at this hour I am dead!
> [...]
> *Guezera*, what great affliction!]

In his lampoon of the melancholic style, Mota employs stereotypes about Jews that a Christian audience would easily recognize as derogatory. The most

---

[36] Marcel Bataillon, '¿Melancolía renacentista o melancolía judía?', in *Varia lección de clásicos españoles* (Madrid: Gredos, 1964), pp. 39–54. For studies of Jewish expressions in Manuel's speech, see Vasconcellos, *Farsa*, pp. 35–44; Paul Teyssier, *La Langue de Gil Vicente* (Paris: Klincksieck, 1959), pp. 202–05; Miller, *Obras*, pp. 265–66; and Luis M. Girón Negrón, '"Juro al Deu aí somos nós": Some Notes on Gil Vicente's Jews and the Spanish and Portuguese *Cancione[i]ros*', *La Corónica*, 40.1 (Fall 2011), 243–93 (pp. 258–59).

obvious stereotypes are those of pride and avarice.[37] The stereotype of the Jew's excessive love of money is clearly at play in Manuel's account of his loss:

> Hum cruzado que poypey,
> em que tanto me rreuia,
> tantas vezes o olhey,
> até que nam no achey (ll. 121–24)
>
> [A *cruzado* that I saved,
> in which I so often saw myself,
> many times I watched it,
> until I was not able to find it]

He also cries:

> Oo cruzado! minha vida!
> pera que te conheçy,
> poys tua triste partida
> me causa dor tam creçida,
> qual eu nunca padeçy? (ll. 56–60)
>
> [O *cruzado*, my life,
> why did I know you,
> since your sad departing
> causes me such great pain,
> the likes of which I have never suffered?]

I would argue that, in these two passages, the author intends an illusion to Narcissus, the conceited mythological figure who died pining after his own image, which he saw reflected in a pool of water. Manuel does say that he saw his reflection in this gold coin (l. 122), and, at one point, he clearly wants to die, pining for his lost *cruzado*:

> Ay, que quero abafar!
> ay, que me quero perder!
> quero-m'yr lançar no mar!
> milhor he de me matar
> que sempre proue viuer!
> O quem me desse ssaber
> onde hum toyro estiuesse!
> hy-lo-hya cometer:
> jur'em Deu, em me comer
> grande graça me fizesse (ll. 21–30)
>
> [Oh, I want to choke!
> Oh, I want to disappear!
> I want to go throw myself into the sea!
> Life always proves
> that I'm better off dead!

---

[37] Previous scholars who have noted (albeit in passing) Mota's use of the stereotype of Jewish avarice include Rocha, *Esboços Dramáticos*, p. 37; and Miller, *Obras*, p. 252.

> Oh, who would tell me
> where I could find a bull?
> I would go offer myself to it:
> by God, it would be doing me a great favour
> in devouring me.]

Mota likely intends for us to make this connection with Narcissus since he mentions him by name earlier in the dialogue:

> D'outra parte namhe ssyso
> buscar minha perdiçam,
> que, quando culpam Narçyso,
> que morreo por mao auiso,
> pois de mym ja, que diram? (ll. 31–35)
>
> [On the other hand, it is not wise
> to seek out my own perdition,
> for, seeing how they fault Narcissus,
> who died by his own bad judgment,
> what will they say about me?]

The next major stereotype developed by Mota is that of the wandering Jew.[38] As is well known, exile has been inextricably linked to Jewish history as far back as the Old Testament wanderings of the tribes of Israel in search of the Promised Land. Christian writers, moreover, commonly described the Jews as damned wanderers punished with exile for the sin of deicide. Pope Innocent III, for instance, likens Jews to Cain, another eternal wanderer, in his bull *Ut esset Cain*.[39] Mota was definitely familiar with the stereotype of the wandering Jew, since he makes direct mention of it in another of his works.[40] And in our text, Manuel makes many references to his state of exile. For example, he cries:

> Mas yr-m'ey por essa terra,
> como homem ssem ventura,
> porqu'a dor que me desterra
> me fará tam crua guerra,
> que moyra ssem sepultura (ll. 11–15)
>
> [But I shall wander through this land,
> as a man without fortune,

---

[38] Mota's use of this stereotype is briefly acknowledged in Faingold, 'Judíos y conversos', p. 42.
[39] Edited and translated in Solomon Grayzel, *The Church and the Jews in the XIIIth Century* (New York: Hermon Press, 1966), pp. 126–27.
[40] *The Lawsuit of Vasco Abul*, l. 296: 'Janes Pera Deos também | sabe muito desta dança' [João de Espera em Deus also | knows a great deal about that dance] (Mateus, *Obras*, p. 89). For studies of the Christian legend of the Wandering Jew (who was named João de Espera em Deus in the form that reached Portugal), see George Kumler Anderson, *The Legend of the Wandering Jew* (Providence, RI: Brown University Press, 1965); Marcel Bataillon, 'Peregrinaciones españolas del judío errante', in *Varia lección de clásicos españoles*, pp. 81–132; Carolina Michaëlis de Vasconcellos, 'O Judeu Errante em Portugal', *Revista Lusitania*, 1 (1887–99), 34–44; and most recently François Delpech, 'De David Reubeni au Juif Errant: dans les pas du "Juif au soulier"', *Revue de l'histoire des religions*, 229.1 (2012), 53–84.

> for the pain which kindles my exile
> will provoke in me such cruel war,
> that I shall die without a sepulchre.]

This exile could be interpreted by a Christian audience as the typical state of the damned, wandering Jew.

However, one important hint suggests that our author does not himself agree with the judge's condemnation of the convert in the play: Mota named the judge after his own father, Gonçalo da Mota, and, according to two documents discovered by Miller in the chancery of João II, his father acted as a municipal judge in 1486 and was fined 500 *reais* because he gave an erroneous judgment during his term.[41] By naming his judge after a person who, as some audience members would know, had given a false verdict, our author is calling into question the Old Christian judge's ruling in the play.

Allegorical Reading (Sympathy for the *Converso*?)

This brings us to the alternative, allegorical and more sympathetic reading of the Jew's exile and wandering in this text, a reading that may be partly informed by tenets of the Maimonidean school of rabbinical tradition regarding the Talmudic penalty for apostasy. This penalty is exclusion from the Jewish community and destruction in the world to come.[42] At the end of days, upon the gathering of the exiled diaspora, apostates will be excluded from redemption and instead subjected to perpetual torment: 'hell shall pass away, but they shall not pass away'.[43] This traditional belief — that perpetual exile from the people of Israel (i.e., excommunication) was the punishment for abjuring God — continues to be seen in writings more contemporary to Mota's period. The fifteenth-century Rabbi Joel ibn Shuaib (of Aragonese origin, living in Navarre) wrote in his *Nora Tehilot* [Awesome in Splendour] that the only future of converts is to rot forever in the 'prison of exile'. When the day of redemption comes, 'God will reject them with both hands'.[44]

Alongside this traditional Talmudic punishment, the fifteenth century witnessed the production of a number of works by Jewish mystics concerning the kabbalistic doctrine of *metempsychosis* (transmigration of the soul). This doctrine had already been expounded in earlier kabbalistic texts such as the thirteenth-century *Sefer ha-Zohar* [The Book of Splendour], which outlines the various stages of the soul's exile. It received renewed importance in the

---

[41] ANTT, *Chancelaria de D. João II*, book 20, fol. 129[r-v]; book 20, fol. 188[r-v]; transcribed in Miller, 'Henrique', pp. 510–12.; see Miller, 'Henrique', pp. 187–88 and 364.

[42] (b=Baylonian Talmud) *bRosh Hashana* 17a; Maimonides, *Hilkhot 'Avodat Kokhavim*, 2. 5; *Hilkhot Mamrim*, 3. 2; *Hilkhot Teshuvah*, 3. 6. 9; see discussion in Benzion Netanyahu, *The Marranos of Spain from the Late XIVth to the Early XVIth Century according to Contemporary Hebrew Sources*, rev. 3rd edn (Ithaca, NY: Cornell University Press, 1999), p. 17 note 47.

[43] *bRosh Hashana* 17a; see also (t-Tosefta) *tSanh*. 13. 5; Maimonides, *Hilkhot Teshuvah*, 3. 6.

[44] Joel ibn Shuaib, *Nora Tehilot* (Salonica: the printing house of Yosef ben Yitzḥaq ben Yosef Ya.vetz, 1568–69), p. 198a; trans. by Netanyahu, *Marranos of Spain*, pp. 174–75.

early fifteenth century, however: in response to the Sophist bent arising among many Spanish Jews, who abandoned the idea of Providence and voluntarily converted amid social pressure in 1412–15, Shem-Tov ben Shem-Tov wrote *Sefer ha-Emunot* [The Book of Beliefs], in which he further developed the theory of metempsychosis in his aim to renew faith in the ideas of Provenance and Punishment and Reward.[45]

Significantly, the *Zohar* is believed to be drawn upon in the writings of one of Mota's contemporaries: Bernardim Ribeiro (c. 1482–1552?). Many details regarding Ribeiro's life are shrouded in mystery. Nevertheless, it has been argued — based on the scant biographical information that can be gathered from his poetry and from mentions of him in two works by Francisco Sá de Miranda (1481–1558) — that the poet and courtier Ribeiro had converted to Christianity voluntarily, likely for material gain, and that, on account of being a crypto-Jew, he fell out of favour at the Portuguese court by 1521 and sought refuge in Italy.[46] Building on comments first made by José Teixeira Rego, scholars such as Helder Macedo and Luís Nepomuceno thus view Ribeiro's eclogues as *prantos* written from the perspective of a crypto-Jew influenced by the ideas of Hispanic kabbalah.[47] They interpret the convert's grief and state of wandering in these enigmatically autobiographical poems as a reference to the kabbalistic notions of exile and union with God as expressed in the *Zohar* and other mystical writings, and it is interesting for our purposes that, as Leite de Vasconcellos first noted, there are striking similarities between the wording of Manuel's *pranto* and the eclogues.[48]

These similarities may well be coincidental, particularly since, though the exact chronological relationship between Mota's farce and Ribeiro's eclogues or his *Menina e Moça* remains unknown, the latter works are suspected to

---

[45] See Netanyahu, *Marranos*, pp. 116–18. For a recent overview of rabbinical writings during this historical period, see also Miriam Bodian, *Dying in the Law of Moses: Crypto-Jewish Martyrdom in the Iberian World* (Bloomington: Indiana University Press, 2007), pp. 1–22.

[46] Helder Macedo, 'A Sixteenth-Century Portuguese Novel and the Jewish Press in Ferrara', *European Judaism: A Journal for the New Europe*, 33.1, The Exile of Jerusalem which is in Sepharad (Spring 2000), 53–58 (pp. 54–55); 'Bernardim Ribeiro', *Dicionário de Literatura Portuguesa*, ed. by Álvaro Manuel Machado (Lisbon: Presença, 1996), pp. 416–17.

[47] José Teixeira Rego, *Estudos e Controvérsias* (Porto: Faculdade de Letras, 1931; repr. Lisbon: Assírio & Alvim, 1991); Helder Macedo, *Do Significado Oculto da Menina e Moça*, 2nd edn (Lisbon: Guimarães, 1999). Macedo's approach was, at first, well received in Jewish scholarship: Gérard Nahon, Review of *Do Significado Oculto da Menina e Moça*, by H. Macedo, *Revue des études juives*, 138 (Jan–Jun 1979), 170–71. In 1977, the Lisbon Academy of Science awarded him the Casimiro Dantas Prize for this study and, though his theories were later attacked by a series of Portuguese and Jewish scholars, the majority of these objections have been successfully refuted by Macedo and more recently by Luís Nepomuceno: Helder Macedo, 'The Strangers Within', *Portuguese Studies*, 13 (1997), 127–29; 'Sixteenth-Century Portuguese Novel', p. 57. For discussion of the objections since negated, see Luís André Nepomuceno, 'Platonism and Judaism: The Theme of *Saudade* in the Eclogues of Bernardim Ribeiro', *Portuguese Studies*, 27.2 (2011), 121–37 (p. 124). Though Herman Prins Salomon is not entirely convinced by Macedo's argument, he nevertheless accepts the possibility of a kabbalistic reading: 'O que Tem de Judaico a *Menina e Moça*?', *Cadernos de Estudos Sepharditas*, 4 (2004), 185–223 (pp. 214–17).

[48] Vasconcellos, *Farsa*, p. 38 note to ll. 46–47. The similarities between Ribeiro's eclogues and Manuel's *pranto* will be further discussed in Matheson, *The Polemics of Conversion*.

have been written afterward, once Ribeiro was already in exile in Italy.[49] The theme of exile and wandering is, moreover, common in Portuguese poetry of the Renaissance period. However, as Nepomuceno has shown, this theme was adopted in an amplified form by Jewish and New Christian authors, and it is no doubt an overpowering aspect of Manuel's lament as well.[50] Exile does not appear to be a prevalent theme in the poems by Ribeiro printed in the *Cancioneiro Geral* — these follow immediately after Mota's at fols 211^r-12^r. One might nevertheless note a similar theme of loss in Ribeiro's *vilancete* with the *incipit* 'Com quantas cousas perdi'. More significantly, as Stephen Reckert has stated, Ribeiro 'characteristically modulates through regret and disillusionment to a resigned expectation of the worst' in his *vilancete* beginning 'Antre mim mesmo e mim'. And the poems beginning 'D'esperança em esperança' and 'esperança minha, is-vos' contain 'nostalgic signifiers — parting and pain, disillusion and loss of hope, loss even of self'. These signifiers suggest to Reckert that, in Ribeiro's early poems, which were not necessarily informed by kabbalah as his eclogues were, one also sees a 'covert allegory of the plight of Iberian Jewry'.[51]

The extent of Mota's contact with Ribeiro is uncertain. One might speculate that, as contemporary poets and courtiers, they might have crossed paths and even exchanged works. Yet Ribeiro, a native of Alentejo, is believed to have been situated at the court in Lisbon whereas Mota's office was in the nearby area of Óbidos, and the latter's writings and biographical details indicate that he was more closely associated with D. Leonor's artistic circle. They may have been connected through common acquaintances: if Mota knew the renowned humanist and translator of Graeco-Latin texts, João Roiz (Rodrigues) de Sá de Meneses (*c*. 1487–1579) — to whom he addresses one of his poems — personally, this may have put him in touch with one of Meneses's close friends, the poet and ardent Erasmian Francisco Sá de Miranda (1487–1558), himself a close friend of Ribeiro's.[52] He thus may have at the very least been connected indirectly with Ribeiro, but one can only speculate about this.

Also, though it is believed that the *Zohar* circulated widely among Sephardic Jews and that it remained popular among converts in fifteenth- and sixteenth-century Spain and Portugal,[53] it would seem far-fetched and unnecessary to argue that our Old Christian Mota engaged directly with this or other Hebrew texts. Though Mota's depiction of the psychological anguish of a convert is

---

[49] Nepomuceno, 'Platonism and Judaism', p. 128.
[50] Luís André Nepomuceno, 'Literatura e Exílio: Cristãos-Novos na Renascença Portuguesa', *Anuario de Letras* (Mexico), 40 (2002), 343–57; Nepomuceno, 'Platonism and Judaism', p. 126.
[51] Stephen Reckert, *From the Resende Songbook*, Papers of the Medieval Hispanic Research Seminar, 15 (London: Department of Hispanic Studies, Queen Mary and Westfield College, 1998), pp. 22 and 28–29; Dias, *Cancioneiro Geral*, pp. 226–28.
[52] 'D'Anrique da Mota a João Roiz de Sá para que falasse por ele ao Conde seu sogro e a Jorge de Vasconcelos seu cunhado sobre dinheiro que lhe não pagavam de vinhos que lhe vendeu para uma armada' (Mateus, *Obras*, p. 31); Macedo, 'Sixteenth-Century Portuguese Novel', p. 54; 'Strangers Within', p. 128.
[53] Luís André Nepomuceno, '"De Mim Mesmo Sou Inimigo": Exílio e Saudade na Écloga II de Bernardim Ribeiro', *Caligrama*, 16.1 (2011), 65–86 (p. 79); 'Platonism and Judaism', p. 134.

unmistakably akin to Ribeiro's poetic works, it seems more likely that Mota would have been drawing upon the Maimonidean punishment for apostasy since, as shall be noted below, its most basic tenets circulated widely among converts and Christians through word of mouth. Nevertheless, it is interesting that one can employ a line of inquiry somewhat similar to that first used by Macedo and read Mota's farce from the perspective of Jewish eschatological tradition.

We might thus return to the above-cited example of one of Manuel's many references to his state of wandering (ll. 11–15), and interpret it in a Talmudic light as an allusion to spiritual exile — to his excommunication from the Jewish community — especially in his statement that he will die without a sepulchre. Manuel makes direct reference to his being in God's disfavour when he says 'Jur'em Deu, que nam me guabe' [By God, who does not applaud me].[54] The God he refers to here is that of his ancestors: here and elsewhere, he pronounces *Deus* [God] without the final –s as many Iberian Jews did in order to eliminate any insinuations of a plural meaning and thereby differentiate their God from the Trinity of the Christians.[55] Only in his prayer to the Holy Spirit does he refer to God with a final –s: 'de ty, Ssenhor, me he dito | que es hum Deos infinito' [I have been told | that you are an infinite God].[56]

The pathos of the text is centred, I would argue, on the remorse and alienation that a *meshumad* feels for having converted voluntarily, distinguishing him from those who resisted and were forcibly converted. According to the rabbinical *responsa* literature of Maimonides and his followers, conversions resulting from coercive measures such as those employed by D. Manuel did not qualify as forced since, in theory, the converts had the option to leave the country of persecution and retain their religion (though of course we know that, in fact, many were prohibited from leaving); forced conversions were those made upon imminent threat of death.[57] Although some rabbinical authors did express more lenient views in which any duress, including financial or social, was sufficient to justify a forced conversion, the authors contemporary to the 1497 conversion were by no means so flexible.

In fact, in their commentaries concerning the 1497 mass conversions, authors such as Isaac Caro and Abraham Saba considered martyrdom the only course to be followed when the alternative was forced conversion, stating that 'compulsion is also will'. According to Caro and Saba, there was no such thing as an *anus* of the 1497 nation-wide conversion.[58] However, the traditional dichotomy does prevail in some writings concerning the converts of 1497,[59] and

---

[54] Vasconcellos, *Farsa*, l. 88.
[55] Vasconcellos, *Farsa*, ll. 9 and 29; Teyssier, *Langue*, pp. 218–19; Salomon, 'O que Tem de Judaico', p. 208.
[56] Vasconcellos, *Farsa*, ll. 143–44.
[57] Netanyahu, *Marranos*, pp. 13–17.
[58] Netanyahu, *Marranos*, pp. 157–74. I am grateful to Dr Nadezda Koryakina for directing me to this important body of literature.
[59] Netanyahu, *Marranos*, pp. 212–15.

those who converted under similar conditions of social and financial duress in Spain in 1412-15 were generally regarded as apostates.[60] Manuel's conversion is clearly presented as apostasy since it is done *de grado* [willingly] (l. 49).[61]

Our author may well have been familiar with the aforementioned rabbinical distinction between voluntary *meshumadim* and forced *anusim* since knowledge of it reached Christian circles throughout the Iberian Peninsula as well. For instance, an explanation of the traditional rabbinical dichotomy is found in a Christian polemic text: the anonymous, late fifteenth-century pamphlet *El libro del alboraique*, which is directed against Judaizing converts. This pamphlet clearly states that *meshumadim* (those who, like Manuel, turned Christian 'de grado') were shunned and thus ostracized by other Jews:

> Desto tomaron entre sí un sobre nombre, en hebrayco hanuzym, que quiere dezir forzados, y si alguno se tornó christiano de grado, y guardava la ley christiana, llamábanle mesumad en hebrayco, que quiere dezir rebolvedor que los revuelve con los xrianos. Y si alguno deste linage llega algún lugar a donde hay aquesta generación, pregúntanle: ¿eres anus, e dest christiano, o mesumad, christiano por la voluntad? Y si responde, christiano soy, anus soy, danle dávidas y hónrranle, y si dice mesumad, no le hablan más.

> [Those baptized by force] took on a nickname, *anusim* in Hebrew, meaning 'forced ones', and if one became Christian voluntarily and observed Christian law, they called him *meshummad* in Hebrew, which means 'turncoat' because he turns against them with the Christians. And if someone of [Jewish] descent arrives at a place where there are people of this generation, they ask him: 'are you *anus*, and in this way a Christian, or *meshumad*, a Christian by choice?' And if he responds, 'I am Christian, I am *anus*', they give him offerings and honour him, and if he says *meshumad*, they speak to him no further.[62]

The text, which enjoyed wide, popular circulation, particularly in the sixteenth century, is believed by Pilar Bravo Lledó and Miguel Fernando Gómez Vozmediano to have been written in Llerena *c.* 1454-74 (before the Inquisition and approximately seventy years after the violence of 1391). The author, they argue, may have been a sincere convert from Judaism who sought to decry and distance himself from Judaizing converts.[63] An earlier argument put forward

---

[60] Netanyahu, *Marranos*, pp. 95-134.
[61] The reading of the farce that I present above is largely dependent on the interpretation of Manuel's statement 'Oxalá que fôra batalha!' (l. 89) as referring to his wish to have more honourably converted as a forced one (*anus*) rather than voluntarily, reflecting the same *anusim/meshumadim* dichotomy described in the *Libro del alboraique*. An alternative reading, equally valid, is that Manuel's conversion, done *de grado*, is reflective of the argument presented by Caro and others that compulsion is will, without reference to an *anusim/meshumadim* dichotomy. This would also place the composition of the farce after 1497, but it would seem more difficult to explain how our Old Christian author could have been familiar with the content of these more recent writings.
[62] Nicolás López Martínez, 'Appendix IV. *Libro llamado El alboraique*', in *Los judaizantes castellanos y la Inquisición en tiempos de Isabel la Católica*, Publicaciones del Seminario Metropolitano de Burgos, Series A, vol. 1 (Burgos: Imprenta de Aldecoa, 1954), pp. 391-404 (p. 391).
[63] Pilar Bravo Lledó and Miguel Fernando Gómez Vozmediano, 'El alborayque: un impreso

by Isidore Loeb offers, based on internal evidence, the more precise date of 1488, during the Inquisition. Loeb suggests that the author intended to deflect inquisitorial attention away from northern kingdoms and towards the sinful southerners.[64] Notably, the term *alboraique* (or *alboraico*) circulated elsewhere in fifteenth-century Spanish writings and in the popular tongue as a derogatory word for *conversos*.[65]

Whether or not Mota had come into direct contact with these Spanish writings or the insult *alboraique*, the social and spiritual repercussions of apostasy would certainly have been a topical subject for discussion between Old and New Christian neighbours in Portugal. Inquisitorial records indicate that some forced converts had been quite vocal in expressing displeasure over their spiritual predicament.[66] Familiarity with the classical dichotomy of *anusim* and *meshumadim*, as expounded by Maimonides, could thus well have been transmitted by word of mouth. We know, moreover, from João de Alcobaça's *Speculum hebraeorum* (1333) that, historically, Jewish teachings were spread orally, for instance in public squares, which were a popular arena for disputes between defenders of Christian and Jewish doctrine.[67] Later, measures aimed at enforcing the social integration of Old and New Christians were introduced by D. Manuel after 1497, and many public offices from which Jews had formerly been barred were now accessible to them.[68] While this may theoretically have increased the chances for Mota's own interaction with New Christian peers, evidence of Jewish and New Christian medical doctors in D. Leonor's court may offer a slightly more concrete channel of influence.

The queen is known to have kept certain Jewish and New Christian physicians in her employ, including Mestre João de Mazagão (also known as Mestre João da Paz).[69] Mota is moreover known to have socialized with at least one of D. Leonor's doctors. His aforementioned work known as *The Lawsuit of*

panfletario contra los conversos fingidos de la Castilla tardomedieval', *Historia, instituciones, documentos*, 26 (1999), 57–83.

[64] Isidore Loeb, 'Polémistes chrétiens et juifs en France et en Espagne', *Revue des études juives*, 18 (1889), 43–70 and 219–42 (pp. 238–42). See also David M. Gitlitz, 'Hybrid Conversos in the "Libro llamado El alboraique"', *Hispanic Review*, 60.1 (Winter 1992), 1–17.

[65] López, *Los judaizantes*, p. 53; María Elena Martínez, *Genealogical Fictions: Limpieza de Sangre, Religion, and Gender in Colonial Mexico* (Stanford, CA: Stanford University Press, 2008), p. 164.

[66] For some examples of alleged complaints voiced by New Christian Maria Rodrigues, as reported by her neighbours and contained in ANTT, *Inquisição de Lisboa, Livro 1 de denúncias*, see Soyer, *Persecution*, pp. 288–89.

[67] For a full discussion, see Mário Martins, 'A Filosofia Esotérica no "Speculum hebraeorum"', in *Estudos de Literatura Medieval* (Braga: Livraria Cruz, 1956), pp. 349–58 (p. 356). See also Bodian, *Dying in the Law*, pp. 12–13.

[68] José Pedro Paiva, 'The New Christian Divide in the Portuguese-Speaking World (Sixteenth to Eighteenth Centuries)', in *Racism and Ethnic Relations in the Portuguese-Speaking World*, ed. by Francisco Bethencourt and Adrian Pearce (Oxford: Oxford University Press, 2012), pp. 269–80 (p. 273–74).

[69] Maria José Ferro Tavares, *Judaísmo e Inquisição: Estudos* (Lisbon: Presença, 1987), p. 46; *Grande Enciclopédia Portuguesa e Brasileira*, ed. by António Mendes Correia et al., vol. xx (Lisbon: Editorial Enciclopédia, 1960), s.v. Paz (João da), pp. 700–01.

Vasco Abul contains a section allegedly composed by *ajudadores* [helpers], and nine out of these ten helpers have been identified by Ivo Carneiro de Sousa: all are officials and/or noblemen (and one lady-in-waiting) in D. Leonor's court, including her physician, Mestre Gil.[70] Though there is considerable disagreement as to whether these helpers composed their own pieces, simply read them out loud, or were part of the intended audience,[71] Mota's inclusion of Mestre Gil in this work suggests that he engaged with this physician and quite possibly others as well, some of whom would have been Jews or *conversos*.

By the date Mota's farce was written, the Inquisition in Spain had already been investigating the faith of Jewish converts (including descendants of the 1391 forced conversions) for approximately two decades. Forced conversions had, moreover, recently been undertaken in Portugal by D. Leonor's husband, João II, in his handling of the Castilian exiles of 1492: those who entered the kingdom seeking only temporary shelter were obliged to leave within a set time limit (eight months, according to Rui de Pina),[72] but many migrants had been unable to leave, either because they were unable to board the ships within the prescribed time or because they were unable to afford the exorbitant prices that the captains demanded for passage. They were reduced to servitude and, in 1493, their children were taken from them, baptized, and sent to populate the new-found island of São Tomé.[73] The 'Jewish problem' was once again a matter of current interest in D. Manuel's reign, and had Mota engaged in conversation with his peers regarding the eschatological ramifications of apostasy he could be drawing on the Jewish perspective gained from these dialogues in his depiction of Manuel.

Meshumad, participle of the verb *shamad*, literally means 'someone destroyed' or 'someone dead',[74] and it would thus appear that Mota presents his convert as a repentant *meshumad* from the very first line of the dialogue with 'Woe, that I am destroyed!'. He continues:

> Oh, Adonai [the Hebrew word for God], what will I do!
> Because I willed my sin [likely a reference to his conversion]
> I have lost my *cruzado*
> [...]
> for at this hour I am dead! [again, a translation of *meshumad*][75]

---

[70] Sousa, *Rainha D. Leonor*, pp. 180 and 841–88.
[71] For a summary of these arguments, see Villalva, *Vasco Abul*.
[72] Rui de Pina, *Crónica de D. João II*, ed. by Luís de Albuquerque (Lisbon: Publicações Alfa, 1989), pp. 135–39 (chapter 65).
[73] Garcia de Resende, 'Vida e Feitos d'el Rey Dom João Segundo', *Livro das Obras de Garcia de Resende*, ed. by Evelina Verdelho (Lisbon: Fundação Calouste Gulbenkian, 1994), pp. 147–456 (pp. 418, chapter 179); François Soyer, 'King João II of Portugal "O Príncipe Perfeito" and the Jews (1481–1495)', *Sefarad*, 69.1 (Jan-Jun 2009), 75–99.
[74] Avraham Even-Shoshan, *Milon Even Shoshan. Even Shoshan Dictionary* (Hebrew), 6 vols, rev. edn (Jerusalem: The New Dictionary; ha-Milon he-ḥadash, 2003), III, 1124; VI, 1912; Philip S. Alexander, 'Insider/Outsider Labelling and the Struggle for Power in Early Judaism', in *Religion, Language, and Power*, ed. by Nile Green and Mary Searle-Chatterjee (New York: Routledge, 2008), pp. 83–100 (p. 89).
[75] Vasconcellos, *Farsa*, ll. 1–10, cited above.

This farce is not really about a stingy Jew who overreacts to the loss of a single coin; it is an allegory of the loss of one's religious identity: Manuel lost the gold coin that he saw himself reflected in. His image is, according to the Old Testament, the image of God, so, on an allegorical level, we might say that he is lamenting his Godless state as an outcast soul and trying to obtain justice for the fact that he was made to suffer this loss in the first place.

Of course, in addition to the above-described reading informed by Jewish doctrine, one must also consider the possibility of a reading informed by Christian tradition concerning apostasy. Such a reading might also view the convert's statements that he is dead (ll. 1, 10) as reflective of the punishment for abjuring God described in Deuteronomy 13: the apostate is to be killed. As the famous fourteenth-century exegete Nicholas of Lyra explains in his moral reading of Deuteronomy, this death is at first symbolic, signifying the apostate's banishment or exclusion from the Christian community, taking the form of excommunication, his eschatological death. (If he continues in perfidy, however, he will be subject to physical death.)[76] This explanation is in accordance with Church law, which traditionally punished apostates with excommunication, and in this Christian vein we can also read Manuel's multiple references to his state of exile.[77] The statement that Manuel will die without a sepulchre (l. 15) may thus moreover also be interpreted in a Christian sense as a reference to the fact that apostates and other excommunicates were traditionally denied a Christian burial — a tradition attested as far back as Pope Leo the Great's letter to Rusticus, Bishop of Gallia Narbonensis [we cannot be in communion with those, when dead, with whom when alive we were not in communion],[78] and which is still seen in the old Roman Ritual VI. 2, *De iis quibus neganda est ecclesiastica sepultura* [On those to whom a Christian burial is denied]. The tradition is also mentioned in canon law texts such as Boniface VIII's *Liber sextus* (Bonif. 5, 2, 2) on the desecration of the graves of those discovered to be heretics post-burial: 'And that place shall always lack a sepulchre'.[79] In all these early discussions, apostates fall under the category of heretics, and in this *Liber*

---

[76] Sebastian Brant (ed.), *Biblia latina cum glossa ordinaria ... et cum postillis ac moralitatibus Nicolai de Lyra* (Basel: Johann Froben and Johann Petri de Langendorff, 1498), fol. 346ʳ: 'Per istum prophetam falsum qui precipitur interfici significantur omnes diuinatores et doctores superstitiosi qui primo sunt occidendi spirituali gladio per excommunicationem. Et si permanserint obstinati dimittendi sunt iusticie seculari occidendi per mortem corporalem'.

[77] *Liber extra* (Greg. 5, 7, 7-10; Greg. 5, 9); Concilium Lateranense IV (c. 3); see also Thomas Aquinas, *Summa theologica* (Sum. II-II, Q. 12, Art. 2).

[78] Leo the Great, Gregory the Great, trans. by Charles Lett Feltoe, ed. by Philip Schaff and Henry Wace, repr. edn of Nicene and Post-Nicene Fathers, Series II, Volume 12 (Peabody, MA: Hendrickson, 1995), p. 111; 'Sancti Leonis Magni Romani Pontificis Epistolae', in *Opera Omnia Leonis Magni*, ed. by J.-P. Migne, Patrologia Latina, 54 (Paris: Garnieri Fratres, 1846), cols 582–1213 (cols 1205–06), Epistle 167, response to Question VIII: *De his qui jam deficientes poenitentiam accipiunt, et ante communionem moriuntur*): 'Nos autem quibus viventibus non communicavimus, mortuis communicare non possumus'.

[79] *Corpus iuris canonici: editio Lipsiensis secunda*, ed. by Emil Friedberg and Emil Ludwig Richter, vol. II (Leipzig: Tauchnitz, 1879–81; facs. repr. Union, NJ: Lawbook Exchange, 2000), col. 1070: 'Et locus ille perpetua careat sepultura'.

sextus it is moreover specified that both must receive the same punishment.[80]

In Roman law, the penalty was the loss of one's civil rights (i.e., civil death). The text in Justinian's *Codex* (C. 1, 7 (*de apostatis*), 3, 2) adds:

> And they shall never return to their former condition, the flagitiousness of their morals shall never be obliterated by penitence, or covered up by any pretended and invented excuse or exculpation, since lies and pretenses cannot protect those who have polluted the faith which they had vowed to God, and who, having betrayed the divine mystery, have joined the profane. Help is extended to the fallen and to the erring, but the lost ones, those who have profaned the holy baptism, cannot be aided by any remedy of penitence, which helps other crimes.[81]

This tradition, too, may be reflected in Manuel's despair; the eschatological implications of abjuring one's God would not escape a sensitive audience knowledgeable of Christian conventions concerning apostasy.

Mota was not necessarily schooled in the Romano-canonical legal tradition. Such training was not a prerequisite for the position of judge of orphans, and his works betray no indication of formal legal instruction — apart, of course, from the reference to the Italian jurist Bartolus of Sassoferrato (d. 1357) in a section of *The Lawsuit of Vasco Abul* that may, as some scholars have pointed out, have been written by Gil Vicente (c. 1465–1536/37) in this arguably composite poem.[82] Leonor's was indeed one of the largest libraries in the kingdom, and, if Mota had access to it, he may have consulted Nicolas of Lyra's reading of Deuteronomy since Sousa, in his attempt at constructing a list of her books, has located a 1496 edition of the *Glossa Ordinaria* (with Nicolas's moral and literal readings) from her collection.[83] Though the volume located only covers the Old Testament books of Isaias to Maccabees, it is unlikely that the queen would have acquired an incomplete set. There may be no way of knowing whether her library also included books of canon and Roman law, but certainly the basic tenets of the canonical punishment for apostasy would have been common knowledge among Christians at this period.

---

[80] Bonif. 5, 2, 13.
[81] *Annotated Justinian Code*, trans. by Fred H. Blume, 2nd edn, rev. by Timothy Kearley (2008) <http://www.uwyo.edu/lawlib/blume-justinian/ajc-edition-2/books/> [accessed 3 February 2015]. *Corpus iuris civilis*, vol. 2, *Codex Iustinianus*, ed. by Paul Krüger, 11th edn (Berlin: Weidmann, 1954; repr. 1997), p. 60: 'Sed nec umquam in statum pristinum revertentur, non flagitium morum oblitterabitur paenitentia neque umbra aliqua exquisitae defensionis aut muniminis obducetur, quoniam quidem eos, qui fidem quam deo dicaverant polluerunt et prodentes divinum mysterium in profana migraverunt, tueri ea quae sunt commenticia et concinnata non possunt. Lapsis etenim et errantibus subvenitur, perditis vero, hoc est sanctum baptisma profanantibus, nullo remedio paenitentiae, quae solet aliis criminibus adesse, succurritur'. The same occurs in the earlier *Codex Theodosianus* (16, 7 (*de apostatis*)). On the punishment for apostasy in Manueline Code, see *OM* V. 2, which states that those guilty of apostasy were tried in ecclesiastical courts but incorrigible perpetrators were handed over to the king's jurisdiction so that the latter could carry out sentences that involved corporal punishment.
[82] Mateus, *Obras*, p. 91 ll. 369–70; Villalva, *Vasco Abul*; M. Vieira Mendes, 'Gil Vicente (no *Cancioneiro Geral*)', in *Dicionário de Literatura Medieval Galega e Portuguesa*, ed. by Giulia Lanciani and Giuseppe Tavani (Lisbon: Caminho, 1993), pp. 296–97.
[83] Sousa, *Rainha D. Leonor*, pp. 775, 889 and 897.

Thus, even from a Christian perspective, one can detect a commiserative angle to the depiction of the *converso*'s exile and wandering: the text still portrays an acute understanding of the spiritual implications suffered by a person induced into apostasy for reasons other than religious conviction. Whether Mota was drawing on popular rabbinical tradition or Catholic tradition or both, the sympathetic reading of Manuel's spiritual predicament presented above remains a valid possibility. And despite the viability of the Christian eschatological reading, it is still very possible that Mota's depiction of Manuel's grief is also informed by popular knowledge of the Maimonidean dichotomy between forced and voluntary converts. As seen above, one would suspect this not only because he laments that his conversion was voluntary and not forced (ll. 3, 49, 88), but also because Jewish eschatological tradition would quite logically be invoked since it is the religion from which he has apostatized and since the Jewish God is the one in whose disfavour he claims to be (l. 80).

Apart from the aforementioned fleeting reference to the Wandering Jew, João Espera em Deus, Jewish- or *converso*-related themes do not reoccur in the few other works by Mota that have survived, so one cannot use his other writings to substantiate the above-argued reading informed by Jewish tradition. Similarly, extant sources concerning Mota's biography do not provide any further indication that he opposed forced conversion or empathized with *conversos*.

One can, however, use his other dramatic dialogues to substantiate a sympathetic depiction of the *converso*'s psychological anguish. As Miller and others have shown, two of the other four pieces are known to contain social satire. His piece commonly known as *O Pranto do Clérigo* [The Priest's Lament] has been described as an Erasmian critique of a corrupt clergyman that is done 'in an extremely burlesque manner, using a tone which would not be offensive'.[84] And the more serious piece known as *The Mule's Lament* is considered by Crabbé Rocha, Miller, and Mateus to contain a critique of the actions of royal officials and clergymen during a famine plaguing Portugal — at a time when the Portuguese nation (represented by an emaciated mule) was starving, there was in fact no shortage of food and, according to their reading of the text, the clergy themselves continued to live in plenty.[85] Mota was thus quite adept at using the comedic mode to communicate a serious political statement, and he is also known to have voiced in his works his disapproval of the actions of lay and ecclesiastical figures. It is therefore quite possible that the social satire contained in *The Farce of the Tailor* is actually directed against Manueline policy towards the Jews and not the Jews/*conversos* themselves. Manuel is the embodiment of this Manueline policy (hence, perhaps, Mota's decision to give him the same name as the king), and, through him, Mota shows that even a

---

[84] Miller, 'Henrique', p. 313; *Obras*, pp. 227–51. See also Mota's poem in goliardic style discussed above at note 27.
[85] Mateus, *Obras*, pp. 72 ll. 316–24, 75–76 ll. 434–42, and 15–17; Crabbé Rocha, *Esboços Dramáticos*, pp. 25–26; Miller, *Obras*, pp. 222–23.

Jew who willingly converts as a result of the king's coercive tactics (i.e., even one who represents the best-case scenario, before the violence of the forced baptisms) will not necessarily be a wholehearted Christian.

It would appear that this closer, more compassionate reading did not escape Gil Vicente, the more famous dramatist under D. Leonor's patronage.[86] Vicente was a known defender of New Christians: by means of a letter addressed to João III decrying the monks of Saint Francis in Santarém, he interceded on the New Christians' behalf to prevent a pogrom after the violent earthquake of 1531. (The monks had been propagating the idea that the calamity was a punishment from God, angered by the insincerity of new converts.)[87] And as Luis Girón Negrón has noted, though Jews are typically demonized in Vicente's religious plays, 'the representation of Jews and *conversos* in Vicente's nonreligious works is, nonetheless, singularly warm and sympathetic'.[88] It is suspected that a reference is made to Mota's *Farce of the Tailor* in the incorrect sentence uttered by Vicente's own judge in his farce *O Juiz da Beira* [The Judge of Beira], first performed in 1525.[89] When confronted with a case involving a procuress and an *escudeiro* who seeks to recover his money from her, Vicente's comically ignorant and illiterate judge decrees 'Desde aqui sentenceio eu | a moeda por perdida | como alma de judeu' [I hereby declare | that the coin is lost | like the soul of a Jew].[90] This judge's final sentence is presented as faulty (it suggests that the procuress was legally entitled to her income, thereby denying the fact that procuring was a crime), as are the judge's other sentences in this play.[91] Vicente and Mota, both members of D. Leonor's court, were in the same artistic circle, and we have already seen that Vicente's involvement in *The Lawsuit of Vasco Abul* (whether as co-author, reciter, or audience member) suggests that they were in close contact. It is quite possible that they exchanged written work, and it is even more likely that this familiarity gave Vicente special insight into the intended message in Mota's farce — which message he may have tried to spell out more clearly in his own *Judge of Beira*.

Conclusion

As Mota has shown, coerced conversion is a no-win situation. We see this in the tailor's grief over his spiritual exile, we also see it in the Old Christian judge's verdict: the loss Manuel has suffered through the abjuration of his faith is far greater than the tenuous position he has gained within the Christian community. Moreover, the pressure tactics used by D. Manuel to coerce Jews

---

[86] Mendes, 'Gil Vicente'; Américo da Costa Ramalho, *Estudos sobre a Época do Renascimento* (Lisbon: Fundação Calouste Gulbenkian, 1997), p. 173 note 3.
[87] Gil Vicente, *Obras Completas*, ed. by Marques Braga, 4th edn, 6 vols (Lisbon: Livraria Sá da Costa Editora, 1968), VI, 251–55; recently discussed in Girón, 'Juro al Deu', p. 249.
[88] Girón, 'Juro al Deu', pp. 246–48.
[89] Vasconcellos, *Farsa*, pp. 47–49; Rocha, *Esboços Dramáticos*, pp. 37–38.
[90] Gil Vicente, *Obras Completas*, V, 300 ll. 16–18.
[91] Braga, *Obras*, V, 273.

to convert may have removed Judaism on an official, superficial level, but they have not furthered Christianity since they have not produced wholehearted Christians.[92] This is clear in the *converso*'s prayer to the Holy Spirit, which is an illustration of the caveat outlined in Gratian, D.45 c.5 and Gratian, C.23 q.4 c.17, which state that Jews are not to be led to the faith by force or attrition but by kind example so that their motive for baptism will be nothing other than divine inspiration. Manuel, as demonstrated in his prayer, is clearly not a true Christian follower:

> Ó tu, Ssenhor Ssant'Esprito,
> posto que t'eu nam conheça,
> de ty, Ssenhor, me he dito
> que es hum Deos infinito,
> & m'o metem em cabeça;
> e dizem que m'ofereça
> a ty em mynha paixam (ll. 141–47)
>
> [O you, Holy Spirit,
> although I don't know you,
> I have been told
> that you are an infinite God,
> so they put it in my head;
> and they tell me to offer myself
> to you in my passion]

Most interestingly, the prayer includes the daring statement:

> & posto que me nam creça
> deuaçam quanta mereça,
> nam me ponhas culpa, nam' (ll. 148–50)
>
> [and although devotion does not grow within me,
> not as much as you deserve,
> don't lay the blame on me, don't.]

Whose fault is it then? Clearly, though in the guise of a comedic text deriding a convert, Mota's *Farce of the Tailor* is a biting critique of D. Manuel's actions towards the Jews of his realm in 1496 and following. It is a polemic against coerced conversion, and, upon close examination, it portrays a sympathetic description of the social and spiritual alienation suffered by a convert in Portuguese society at the turn of the sixteenth century. For this reason, and on account of its subtle and deft argumentation, it deserves a place in the larger corpus of polemic literature from the Iberian Peninsula in the early modern period.

My sincere thanks are due to Professor Josiah Blackmore for directing the research presented in this paper and to Professor John Tolan and Dr François Soyer for the

---

[92] For discussion of how D. Manuel himself had 'few illusions about the sincerity of the new converts' and of how Old Portuguese society in general doubted the religious sincerity of the New Christians, see Soyer, *Persecution*, pp. 285–87.

illuminating feedback I received at conferences they organized. I am also grateful for the helpful comments of anonymous reviewers. This research was supported by the Social Sciences and Humanities Research Council of Canada and the European Research Council under the European Union's Seventh Framework Programme (FP7/2007–2013) / ERC grant agreement n° 249416. This publication is part of the research project RELMIN 'The Legal Status of Religious Minorities in the Euro-Mediterranean World (5th–15th centuries)'.

A Newly Discovered Novel and its Transnational Author: *Maria Severn* by Francisca Wood

Cláudia Pazos Alonso

Wadham College, Oxford

In 1874, Lady Catherine Jackson gave an account of her travels through Portugal in *Fair Lusitania*. After briefly expressing her surprise at the lack of contemporary Portuguese women novelists in comparison to England, she mentioned the name of the only writer she had come across, a name veiled by a colourful pseudonym: *Fornarina de Avellar*. When, four years later, Camilo published his translation of Jackson's work as *A Formosa Lusitânia* (1878), he provided additional information in a footnote, so as to satisfy the curiosity of his readers — at least in part. He indicated that the reference 'allude a um romance desconhecido da senhora D. Amelia Dulce de Serpa Pinto, que o escreveu com o pseudonymo de *Fornarina de Avella* [sic]' [alludes to an unknown novel by Mrs Amelia Dulce de Serpa Pinto, which she wrote under the pseudonym of *The Baker-girl of Avella*].[1] For the sake of completeness, he added: 'Simultaneamente escreviam D. Maria Amalia Vaz de Carvalho e D. Guiomar Torresão, das quaes a escriptora ingleza não levou noticia nem informação' [At the same time were writing Maria Amalia Vaz de Carvalho and Guimar Torresão, about whom the English writer gathered no knowledge or information].[2] This anecdotal evidence is telling: firstly, Lady Jackson had not come across any reference to two of the better regarded female writers of the *Geração de 70*, even though Torresão's first novel, *Uma alma de mulher*, had been published in 1869. Secondly, she had not been told either about *Maria Severn* (a novel also published in 1869), as one might perhaps have expected, given that its author, Francisca Wood, was the wife of a British gentleman. Nor, for that matter, was Camilo aware of Wood.[3] And not much seems to have changed in the intervening one hundred and forty years.

---

[1] Catharina Carlota Lady Jackson, *A Formosa Lusitânia*, trans. by Camilo Castelo Branco (Porto: Livraria Portuense, 1878), p. 10. There is no entry for an Amélia Dulce de Serpa Pinto in any dictionary of Lusophone women writers. Her surname, however suggests that she may have been connected with the family of the famous nineteenth-century explorer Serpa Pinto. Indeed, according to a thread on <http://geneall.net/en/forum/21404/serpa-pinto/#a282005>, she was his first cousin.
[2] Ibid.
[3] For a discussion of his omission of the name of his long-term partner/wife, Ana Plácido, from the list, see Pazos Alonso, 'Assimetrias de Género: a trajetória de Ana Plácido e o papel de Camilo', in *Representações do feminino em Camilo Castelo Branco*, ed. by Sérgio Guimarães de Sousa (Braga: Centro de Estudos Camilianos, 2014), pp. 39–63.

Therefore, the present article focuses on the Portuguese journalist Francisca Wood, and her novel *Maria Severn*, initially serialized in the remarkable periodical that she directed for two years, the weekly *A Voz Feminina*, launched in January 1868 and renamed *O Progresso* halfway through 1869, when she became joint director with her British husband, William Thorold Wood.[4] The article was prompted in the first instance by my discovery three years ago of what appears to be the only surviving copy of *Maria Severn* in book form.[5] I am currently preparing a new edition of this novel for publication in Portugal, in a bid to start reversing the fairly generalized neglect of nineteenth-century women's writers in Portuguese cultural memory.

Throughout the nineteenth century, significant cultural transformations occurred in Portugal. As Kathryn Bishop-Sanchez highlights:

> The emergence of a relatively broader reading public [...] the development of means of communication, the greater circulation of culture and knowledge and the growing influence of the press are some of the many aspects that radically changed nineteenth-century life.[6]

As such, the press allowed new opportunities for a new generation of women willing to fight to play a role with greater public visibility. Their writing and literary creations in many cases came out in periodicals, as is demonstrated by Ana Maria Costa Lopes in her in-depth and informative *Imagens da mulher na imprensa feminina de oitocentos: percursos de modernidade* (see note 4). It was fairly common during that period for novels to be published in instalments in newspapers and periodicals, and only subsequently printed in book form — this was the case with several nineteenth-century classics such as Garrett's *Viagens na minha terra*, Dinis' *Uma família inglesa* — and *Maria Severn* is no exception. Its first instalment was published on 19 July 1868, seven months after the launch of *A Voz Feminina*, in number 27. The last instalment, published on 19 December 1869, only stretches to part of Chapter 26 and therefore leaves the serialized version incomplete (with three and a half chapters still to come). In fact, it ends on a cliffhanger. Curiously, the very last number of *A Voz Feminina*, of 26 December 1869, does not include any further instalment, possibly because there was no room. Possibly Francisca Wood thought that an instalment that ended with a cliffhanger was a suitable way to sign off — and might even encourage readers to purchase the book, if they had not done so already.

The book, published in two volumes, became available in early November 1869, a few weeks before the periodical folded.[7] It is not known how many

---

[4] Although these two forward-looking periodicals have already been singled out for their pioneering role in the Portuguese context (see Ana Maria Costa Lopes, *Imagens da mulher na imprensa feminista de oitocentos: percursos de modernidade* (Lisbon: Quimera, 2005)), my current research project seeks to demonstrate their unrivalled importance when examined from a transnational perspective.
[5] Francisca d'Assis Martinz Wood, *Maria Severn*, 2 vols (Lisbon: Tipografia da Voz Feminina, 1869).
[6] Kathryn Bishop-Sanchez, '"The Other Nineteenth Century"?', in The Other Nineteenth Century, *Portuguese Literary & Cultural Studies*, 12 (2007), pp. xiii–xxv (pp. xiii–xiv).
[7] Since women novelists (as opposed to poets, translators, or short story writers) were still a relative

copies were printed but even if it was a modest run the novel was distributed in several Portuguese cities, according to the publicity in O Progresso.[8] Yet, despite my best efforts, so far I have been unable to identify a single copy of *Maria Severn* in any Portuguese public library. This forward-looking novel has simply remained forgotten for nearly 150 years, since even the incomplete serialized version published in *A Voz Feminina* has never been republished.[9] The disappearance of a nineteenth-century novel written by a woman is not unique, but the thrill of discovering a copy of *Maria Severn* in the British Library most certainly was. As I eagerly read it from cover to cover, it soon became apparent that I was dealing with a remarkably innovative text, both in terms of literary style and ideas. In excess of 100,000 words, it is primarily a novel of manners, underpinned by the same progressive political convictions so much in evidence throughout Wood's journalistic work. The novel, wholly set in Britain (between Andover and Newbury, in Hampshire), portrays the British landed gentry, contrasting the traditional Yorks with the progressive Severns. It is set within the wider context of the considerable social changes and unrest that followed the Reform Act of 1832, which led to the widening of male voting rights. As a result, several historians credit the Reform Act with the start of modern democracy in Britain.

As early as Chapter 6, there are allusions to reformers such as Lord John Russell (the principal architect of the 1832 act), Cobden (a radical MP who was associated with the anti-Corn Law league), and the radical reformer Thomas Thompson, who wrote several articles in the well-known Victorian journal *Westminster Review* and supported universal suffrage. This can be seen for instance from the following passage:

> O sacristão, que era o fanqueiro e capitalista da aldeia, lia, apoiado no seu balcão, as notícias aos seus fregueses; o *Catecismo de falácias* do coronel Thompson foi introduzido no vale, lido e discutido e explicado; numa palavra, as grandes medidas parlamentares eram analisadas nos campos, à medida que as sementes caíam na terra. (Vol. 1, Chapter 6)
>
> [The sacristan, who was the draper and the capitalist of the village, was propped up at his counter, reading the news to his customers; Colonel Thompson's *Catechism on the Corn Laws* was introduced into the valley, read and debated and explained; in a word, the great parliamentary measures were analysed in the fields, as the seeds were falling on the ground.]

---

rarity in Portugal, *Maria Severn* bore the label '*romance original*', possibly in order to make clear that it was not a mere translation. Incidentally the aforementioned novels *Uma alma de mulher* (1869), by Guiomar Torresão (with a preface by Júlio César Machado) — also initially serialized in *A Voz Feminina* — *Herança de Lágrimas* (1871), by Ana Plácido, and *Henriqueta* (1876), by Maria Peregrina de Sousa (with a preface by Castilho) are all also called '*romance original*'. The works of some mid-nineteenth-century male writers (e.g. Camilo) were also occasionally so described, but less frequently.

[8] It was distributed in Lisbon, Porto and Braga, according to numbers 95 and 99.

[9] To the best of my knowledge, only one enterprising researcher to date has worked on the serialized version and attempted to assess its worth (see Maria de Deus Duarte, 'Pink Sunsets: Configurações e (Des)figurações em Mary Severn', *Revista de Estudos Anglo-Portugueses*, 14 (2005), 257–82). However, the fact that she was working from an incomplete version of the novel unavoidably affected her conclusions.

Clearly, Wood was familiar with British politics, and a further proof comes from the very copy of *Maria Severn* that I discovered in the British Library, for it bears a handwritten dedication to Charles Wentworth Dilke. Given the dates involved, this must necessarily be the youngest Dilke of that name (1843–1911): elected Liberal MP for Chelsea in 1868 at the age of twenty-five, he went on to become a major Victorian figure.[10] The Dilke family owned one of the most influential periodicals of the Victorian period, *The Athenaeum* and, quite aside from a shared progressive political outlook, the gift to Dilke makes perfect sense because *The Athenaeum* had registered the appearance of *A Voz Feminina* in its 'weekly gossip' column on 6 June 1868, in the following laudatory terms:

> The Female Question is making strange progress. From a city so little likely to be stirred by sentiment as Lisbon we have received several numbers of a paper called *A Voz Feminina*, which is written by ladies and devoted to the cause of woman's emancipation. The chief editor is Madame Francisca D'Assis Martinz Wood, the Portuguese wife of an English gentleman. Space is given to fiction, poetry, musical history, and fashions; the latter being described in French. *A Voz Feminina* would be useful to persons who are studying Portuguese.[11]

Even more unexpectedly, Dilke is mentioned in *O Progresso* (no. 80, p. 1) in an open letter from William Wood to The Editor of *The Printers' Register*, where Wood discusses the gradual progress being made in England regarding the vote for women. He then discloses that a petition for the women's vote was presented by Sir Charles Wentworth Dilke, though it only attracted five signatures. Leaving aside any detailed comment about William's political activism, this piece of information indicates that Francisca Wood's Victorian liberal values were wholeheartedly supported by her British husband. As for the English setting of *Maria Severn*, another open letter by William Wood, this time to Theodore Stanton, reveals that Francisca had lived in England for thirty-five years, prior to her return to Portugal.[12] While more research is required to gain a better understanding of couple's international connections (for instance Stanton was the son of the well-known American feminist activist Elizabeth Stanton and the abolitionist Henry Stanton), there can be no doubt about their first-hand, and indeed ongoing, exposure to British culture and politics over a long period of time. In terms of actual proof of their familiarity with Victorian literature, suffice to say that William was an early publisher of Dickens in Portuguese.[13]

---

[10] For further details about his career, see Roy Jenkins, *Dilke: A Victorian Tragedy* (London: Bloomsbury Reader, 2012). The subject's father and grandfather were also named Charles Wentworth Dilke, but they had died in 1868 and 1864 respectively, in other words prior to the publication of *Maria Severn*.
[11] *The Athenaeum*, 'Weekly Gossip', 6 June 1868, no. 2119, p. 799.
[12] William Wood, 'To Theodore Stanton of the *Revolution*, New York', *A Voz Feminina*, no. 73, 6 June 1869, p. 4.
[13] His home-grown editorial press was responsible for publishing Charles Dickens' *A Christmas Carol* as *Cânticos de Natal* (Lisbon: Tipografia Luso-Britânica de W. T. Wood, 1873). Perhaps more surprisingly, that same year his press also published a translation of Wilkie Collins' 1866 novel, *Armadale*, as *Armadeile*, confirming his interest in contemporary British literature.

As part of my ongoing research, I have been able to gather new information which sheds light on William Thorold Wood (1816–1888).[14] He was born into an upper-class family: his mother, Jane, was the daughter of Sir John Thorold, a baronet whose family seat was Syston Park, in Lincolnshire,[15] while his father, Charles Thorold Wood, was painted with his brother by the society painter, Sir Henry Raeburn.[16] William Wood himself was a musician and composer,[17] and the British Library holds three of his musical compositions, dating from 1840, 1846 and 1848 respectively, the latter setting to music what was at the time an overtly revolutionary religious hymn, The Peoples' Anthem, as it subsequently became known.[18] It is not known how William and Francisca met, but their wedding took place on 17 July 1852 at St Dunstan in the West, a church in Fleet Street, central London. Six years later, in 1858, there is a record of William Wood on the electoral roll, which indicates that he was living in London. Presumably so too was Francisca. Little is known about their relocation to Portugal,[19] but by the time *A Voz Feminina* was launched, on 5 January 1868, they were also sufficiently well-known and regarded for Francisca to have been approached to direct the periodical. Although she initially declined, she was involved from the start, and officially became named as 'redactora principal' from number 4 onwards.[20]

The novelty of *A Voz Feminina* resided in the fact that it claimed to be the first magazine to have the exclusive collaboration of ladies, although the claim was soon dropped.[21] In the course of its first year, Francisca seized

[14] William Wood was baptized on 25 March 1816 in Cumberland (north-west England) and died in 1888.
[15] Other important connections on his mother's side include one of his cousins, who was Bishop of Rochester, according to Ana Maria Costa Lopes ('Religião e género como formas de discriminação no século XIX: o casal Wood, um study case', *Gaudium Sciendi*, revista eletrónica da Sociedade Científica da Universidade Católica Portuguesa, 2 (2012), 51–65, available online at <http://www.ucp.pt/site/resources/documents/SCUCP/GaudiumSciendi/GaudiumSciendi_N2/N2_Artigos_AnaCosta.pdf>). Although she does not give the exact name, Costa Lopes is probably referring to his younger cousin, Anthony Wilson Thorold (1826–1895), who became Bishop of Rochester in 1877.
[16] The picture was auctioned by Christie's in 1995.
[17] His first signed contribution to *A Voz Feminina* is an overview of the history of music, spread over several issues from number 6 onwards.
[18] The word to The Peoples' Anthem were written by Ebenezer Elliott, an anti-Corn Law poet, and can be seen see at <http://www.hymnary.org/text/when_wilt_thou_save_the_people>.
[19] Lopes ('Religião e género') suggests that it was as part of the movement towards the creation of a Lusitanian church. According to H. E. Noyes, *Church Reform in Spain and Portugal: A Short History of the Reformed Episcopal Churches of Spain and Portugal* (London: Cassell, 1897) the movement took off precisely in the years of 1867–68 and was formalized in 1875. This overview does not include any references to the Woods. It is likely that the Woods had in fact relocated to Portugal in the early 1860s. Their marriage certificate indicates that Francisca was born in 1811, and in *A Voz Feminina*, no. 35 (13 September 1868, p. 1) she disclosed that she was born and raised during the first fourteen years of her life in the *freguesia* (parish) of Santos-o-Velho. This suggests that she would have moved to England around 1825 and returned to her country of birth some thirty-five years later, around 1860.
[20] Her husband provides an explanation of the circumstances in which she came to take on the role of director in the aforementioned letter of William to Theodore Stanton.
[21] The magazine had the ongoing support of a core group of women writers, such as a young and dynamic Guiomar Torresão. Wood took steps to generate a strong sense of a supportive community of female readers and writers (as well as men sympathetic to women's emancipation), not least through the correspondence featured in most issues. Yet, according to Lopes ('Francisca de Assis Martins

the opportunity to shape the periodical, whose forward-looking rallying cry became 'A mulher livre ao lado do homem livre' [the free woman, by the side of the free man], from January 1869 (number 51). When, six months later, it was renamed *O Progresso*, and a second motto was added, the equally combative French 'La justice soit faite, coûte que coûte', she stayed on at the helm with her husband as the joint editor.[22] In short, throughout its two-year existence under the leadership of first one and then both Woods, the magazine had a very clear vision, as the couple took it upon themselves to raise awareness in Portugal of the socio-political progress that was being achieved in countries like Britain, France and the United States.[23]

Wood's extensive engagement with mainstream Victorian themes such as education, social class and legal reform, as well as domesticity and evolving gender roles, is clear not only throughout *A Voz Feminina*, but also in *Maria Severn*, a novel that has didactic aims regarding the dissemination of progressive mid-Victorian values to a Portuguese audience. It is also important to note that the novel was published in the immediate aftermath of the Second Reform Act in 1867, which doubled the number of adult men who could vote. So, by setting her work in the context of the Reform Act of 1832, dating back several decades, when a new act had just come into effect, Francisca Wood is implicitly drawing attention to the march of progress. In practice Wood functions as a cultural mediator, in an attempt to provide a modernizing perspective on socio-political issues that were relevant to the backward situation of Portugal in the second half of the nineteenth century. Furthermore, there is no doubt in my mind that her novel is likely to have been inspired not only by Victorian debates but also, to a large extent, by British literary models, especially those of women writers. Therein lies one of its unprecedented novelties.

In the Portugal of the 1860s, one other major writer was also especially familiar with the British literary tradition: Júlio Dinis, owing to family

---

Wood', p. 314), the magazine also met with a refusal to contribute on the part of some renowned intellectuals such as Maria Amália Vaz de Carvalho and Amélia Janny. This statement turns out to be not quite true in the case of Janny, whose poetry went on to be published in no. 19 (p. 4). On the other hand, Vaz de Carvalho, who would have been just over twenty-one at the time, is cited as having declined on the grounds that writing for the press was a male endeavour (see number 25, p.4, where Francisca scolds her attitude). Ana Maria Costa Lopes, 'Francisca de Assis Martins Wood', in *Feminae. Dicionário Contemporâneo*, ed. by Zília Osório de Castro and João Esteves (Lisbon: Comissão para a Cidadania e a Igualdade de Género, 2013), pp. 312–18, online at <http://cid.cig.gov.pt/Nyron/Library/Catalog/winlibimg.aspx?skey=0BC86F59EEEF4B5DA62821F712ACB60E&doc=95065&img=139416>.

[22] She communicated to her readership the imminent changes (see editorial of no. 74). Her intention had been to take a backseat, but in the end she stayed as co-director at the instigation of some of her readers (see editorial of no. 76), in a fitting display of symbolic equality. And as a compromise solution, once renamed *O Progresso*, a clarification in brackets and in very small print was placed below the new title, confirming that it was a 'continuação de *A Voz Feminina*'.

[23] The magazine also followed the common nineteenth-century practice of republishing text from foreign magazines, analysed by Teresa Pinto Coelho in connection with Eça (*Eça de Queirós and the Victorian Press* (London: Tamesis, 2014)). Amongst those mentioned are the *Quarterly Review*, and *The Printers' Register* (see for example Francisca Wood, 'O que se faz lá fora', *O Progresso*, no. 87, 12 September 1869, p. 153).

connections (namely his mother).²⁴ His first novel, *As pupilas do Senhor Reitor*, was reviewed in *A Voz Feminina* by Guiomar Torresão in May 1868, and a dramatized version of it was also performed in Lisbon that year in the Teatro da Trindade. There is a fair chance, then, that Francisca Wood had also come across and read his second work, *Uma família inglesa*, which was serialized in 1867 and published in book form in 1868. But it seems unlikely that her novel was prompted as a direct response to it, since *Maria Severn*'s opening chapter indicates that it was composed in the winter of 1866 — in other words its creation predates the appearance of *Uma família inglesa* in instalments. Nonetheless, given their common proximity with British literary tradition, it would be difficult to think of another novel of manners in 1860s Portugal with which *Maria Severn* might have as many affinities of style. Júlio Dinis, in his well-known essay 'Ideias que me ocorrem', asserted that

> há livros que são monumentos e livros que são instrumentos, [...] para andarem nas mãos de todos, para educarem, civilizarem e doutrinarem as massas. [...] o livro instrumento precisa de ser popular, escrito na linguagem do dia, ao alcance das inteligências da época, de fácil trato, em suma.²⁵

> [there are books that are monuments and books that are instruments, [...] to pass into the hands of everyone, to educate, to civilize and instruct the masses [...] the book as instrument needs to be popular, written in everyday language, within the reach of the minds of the time, easily grasped, in short.]

The didactic value of literature is something that Wood also holds dear to her heart and thus, thematically speaking, one might expect Wood to subscribe to what David Frier has called, in his discussion of *A morgadinha dos canaviais* (1868), an 'Austen-like progression towards enlightenment', that 'feeds into an essentially rational vision of the appropriate actions required in a given context'.²⁶ It must be noted however that, although Wood was also interested in depicting the psychological development of her respective heroine and her suitor — incidentally also named Henrique — she was in fact considerably more forward-looking than Dinis in her reformist agenda. Moreover, she writes with an acute gendered awareness that not everything was as simple or rosy as Dinis ultimately allowed for in his vision of the potential for the positive construction of a better nation. In this significant difference, she may well be indebted to George Eliot, as we shall see in a moment.

---

[24] For further details, see, Carmen da Conceição da Silva Matos Abreu, 'Júlio Dinis — representações romanescas do corpo psicológico e social: influência e interferência da literatura inglesa' (unpublished doctoral thesis, Universidade do Porto, 2010), available online.

[25] Júlio Dinis, 'Ideias que Me Occorrem', in *Inéditos e Esparsos* (Lisbon: Sousa & Almeida, 1910), pp. 27–48 (p. 38).

[26] David Frier, 'The Transition from Romanticism to Realism: Alexandre Herculano, Camilo Castelo Branco and Júlio Dinis', in *A Companion to Portuguese Literature*, ed. by Stephen Parkinson, Cláudia Pazos-Alonso and T. F. Earle (London: Boydell & Brewer, 2009), pp. 120–30 (p. 129).

Maria Severn features two contrasting families belonging to the provincial aristocracy, the Severns and the Yorks, the latter satirized as a rather dysfunctional family. The eponymous twenty-year-old protagonist Maria,[27] the beloved daughter of Rosa and Arthur Severn, is engaged to be married to Henrique York, the son of Celestina and Squire Leofrico Catecumeno York. As can be seen straightaway from the latter's names, Wood is partial in the way she ascribes names to her characters, and there is a fair chance that, in using names for satirical characterization and comic effect, she may be indebted to Dickens (e.g. Scrooge in 'A Christmas Carol').[28]

Maria, on the other hand, is a virtuous, beautiful and intelligent heroine, endowed with Christian values, and her physical beauty reflects her moral qualities. Throughout the novel, not only is she shown to empathize with those less privileged than herself, but her compassion goes hand-in-hand with advocating social reform, following in the footsteps of her father's progressive socio-political convictions. These include providing local schools for those who work his land (something Eça would depict as one of Jacinto's innovations in *A cidade e as serras*, some thirty years later). Not unlike Margaret, the likeable heroine of Elizabeth Gaskell's *North and South* (1855), Maria is also a spirited young woman. On several occasions she stands up to her fiancé Henrique. In one memorable scene, Maria is even prepared to break off her engagement because of their different outlook regarding the importance of social justice. She asks Henrique whether he would ever be prepared to contemplate abolishing firstborn inheritance rights: 'Repugna-me muito que um filho herde tudo, e os outros filhos nada. Desejara que anulasses a morgadia da tua casa' [It greatly offends me that one son should inherit everything, and the other children nothing. I would like you to annul the firstborn inheritance rights on your estate] (Vol. 2, Chapter 1). Although this particular chapter ends on a cliffhanger, as was common practice in Victorian serialized fiction, with the couple in an impasse, they are duly reconciled in the following chapter, mainly thanks to Rosa's timely mediation: as the maternal voice of mature common sense, she skilfully talks her daughter through the fact that her behaviour was rash, and that she must learn to relativize and become more diplomatic. It is also an opportunity for Wood to flesh out the character of Rosa who, up to then, has remained in the background.[29]

---

[27] Also called Mary at various points. This is one of the several inconsistencies that will have to be dealt with by careful editing, and also applies to other characters and even some name places. For the purposes of this article, I have chosen the version which is most frequently used in the novel.
[28] For instance, the medieval resonance of Leofrico may be an oblique reference to Leofric, Earl of Mercia and husband to Lady Godiva (though, as there are several Leofrics in Britain in the eleventh century it is difficult to be sure which one, if any, Wood might have had in mind). Certainly Leofrico Catecumeno's patronizing ways are described early on as feudal, and, as a feminist living in England, Wood may very well have heard and been impressed by the legend of Lady Godiva, a strong-willed woman prepared to ride naked through the streets of Coventry in order to achieve greater social justice from her cruel husband, Leofric.
[29] It would be interesting to compare and contrast the 'maternal' role of Rosa with that of Jenny in

Wood is especially strong in her depiction of female characters, *à la* Jane Austen, with shrewd observations even when they are caricatured, as is the case with Henrique's two sisters, Barbara Bandana and Ramires Romina, presented for the most part as two giggling adolescents. Numerous flaws are attributed to them, including lack of culture and wisdom, but most can be seen as the result of a defective upbringing.[30] One of the sisters, Barbara, falls for a penniless artist from the capital, Lionel Quemmequer, and eventually marries beneath her station. The pairing of Barbara with Lionel provides a gendered inversion of the familiar Austen-like plot where the woman was often rewarded with the marriage of a man of higher social standing, a plot also visible in the ending of *Uma família inglesa*. In so doing, Wood may be building on what had already been portrayed in *North and South* by Elizabeth Gaskell, published in 1855, where the heroine Margaret eventually marries John Thornton, the northern mill owner she had initially dismissed as her inferior in terms of class.

As for Ramires, she becomes unwisely smitten with the local poet Oucatouca (his name *oca touca*, is especially funny given that it was typically women, not men, who were accused of being vacuous airheads). Aside from Quemmequer, his is the only Portuguese surname in the novel, and both were clearly chosen to comically satirize characters of a slightly lower social standing. Unlike Barbara however, Ramires is led on by Oucatouca. Later on in the novel, feeling abandoned when her sister goes to stay in London to pursue her love interest, she tries to run away by disguising herself as man, even going to the lengths of cutting her locks in order to do so. Her plans, however, fail miserably, as she is forced by poor weather to beat a hasty retreat (Vol. 2, Chapter 22). The omniscient narrator is sympathetic, but in a chapter teeming with comic exaggeration, Wood cannot refrain from showing how melodramatic and ineffectual Ramires' actions were, given how ill-prepared she was to face the real world. At the end of the novel, Ramires ends up safely, if somewhat conventionally, by marrying the local doctor, Denis Liche (perhaps a distortion of Leech, given that leeches were much used in early medicine, and the term 'leech' long remained a popular if mildly disrespectful term for a doctor).

Aside from her forward-looking belief in women's independence of mind, reflected in Maria's convictions — and to a lesser extent in Barbara and Ramires, who, despite being flawed characters, at least have minds of their own — Wood believes in the possibility of human perfectibility. Her editorial in the very first number of *A Voz Feminina* is vocal on this matter, describing the aspirations of Portugal as 'a aquisição do saber humano; a superioridade espiritual; a perfectibilidade enfim; essa utopia grandiosa' [the acquisition of human knowledge; spiritual superiority; in short perfectibility; that grandiose utopia]

Uma família inglesa, in terms of smoothing over problems. The basic decency of Arthur Severn is also matched by Mr Whitestone, although clearly the former belongs to a much higher echelon of society.

[30] Their mother, Celestina, often uses words inappropriately, to great comic effect, and she is not the only character to do so. In so doing, there may be a faint echo of Mrs Malaprop's abuse of language in Richard Sheridan's comedy *The Rivals* (1775).

(5 January 1968, p. 1). The possibility of improvement is amply demonstrated by Henrique, who gradually comes to see that his father's conservative outlook is misguided, as well as deeply anachronistic and unpopular. His transformation contrasts with his own earlier authoritarian stance, which came to the fore in Vol. 1, Chapter 15, when he forbade Maria to go and visit Nell Sanders, a young peasant girl, pregnant outside wedlock.

This is one of several subplots in the novel that enable Francisca Wood to tackle social issues, since the ostracizing of Nell was compounded by the fact that her pregnancy had arisen as a result of incest. Wood, however, refuses to condemn the siblings, as their error stems from ignorance: since Nell and Robert were orphaned at a young age and left to fend for themselves, they did not know any better. We, as readers, are thus invited to consider whether or not we can hold the pair accountable for their actions. Given the way their moral development had been stunted, the blame lies more squarely with society than with them.[31] Therefore, while most of the local community refuses to associate with Nell once her pregnancy becomes apparent — even before the identity of the father of her child is known — Maria continues to visit her, encouraged by her cousin, the saintly vicar, Jorge Deile (possibly a Portuguese spelling of Dale). In defiance of the promise made to Henrique, she can be found at Nell's side when she dies, shortly after giving birth. Instructed by Maria and Jorge, Nell dies a good Christian, having sincerely repented of her sins.[32]

As early as Vol. 1, Chapter 3, another unforgettable *vignette* had already allowed Francisca Wood to develop her strong social concerns and portray the ignorance of the rural working class, when Joe Motts, one of the workers on the York estate, reveals that he has bought a woman, Nancy, from her husband. He cannot see why the transaction is invalid and feels utterly cheated when Nancy returns to her husband, Bob Deans. The shocking issue of wife-selling is not as far-fetched as it might seem to the modern reader, and indeed the opening of *The Mayor of Casterbridge* by Thomas Hardy, published nearly two decades later, in 1886 — though admittedly set in the early nineteenth century — famously opens with a drunken wife-selling scene.[33] Curiously, *A Voz Feminina* published news of one such real-life account of wife-selling reported in the British press, which had been sent in by a reader (issue no. 5, 26 January 1868, p. 4). Wood comments, however, that the reader must have seen it in a very old newspaper, since the practice had been outlawed in Britain since the Divorce Act of 1857. In her novel, neither Jorge nor the York family can believe that

---

[31] Incest would famously feature two decades later in Eça's *Os Maias*, albeit in the context of the upper classes. Critics have often interpreted it as reflecting the inbred nature of the Portuguese elite in the late nineteenth century, but the fact that Carlos *knowingly* sleeps with his sister, even after having been told of their kinship, suggests moral weakness. This gives a rather different slant to the issue of individual versus collective responsibility.

[32] Wood presents her characters as Christian, but with as little emphasis on Anglican practices as possible.

[33] See Christine Winfield, 'Factual Sources of Two Episodes in *The Mayor of Casterbridge*', *Nineteenth-Century Fiction*, 25.2 (1970), 224–31.

anyone would be so ignorant as to think that wife-sales were legal, and she uses this as a golden opportunity to push forward her educational agenda.

This subplot resurfaces with dire consequences, when Joe kills his rival, Bob Deans (Vol. 1, Chapter 12). Both were workers on the York's estate, and the supercilious Leofrico Catecumeno York sees Joe's capital punishment as the only way to deal with the problem. The progressive side, with the vicar Jorge in the lead, attempts to establish the actual circumstances surrounding Bob Deans' death, hoping to have the charges against Joe reduced to manslaughter. As a result, when later in the novel Joe is tried (in a trial which affords a detailed yet simultaneously hilarious description of the proceedings), justice is indeed done. After it transpires that he was provoked by Bob and Nancy, Joe is released, unlike Nancy, who is found guilty of bearing false witness, albeit at the instigation of Oucatouca. She and two other witnesses, who committed perjury as a result of Squire York's bribery, are jailed. If the truth emerges on cross-examination, a sign of Wood's faith in the fairness of the justice process in British courts, there is nonetheless widespread discontent, as the three witnesses are perceived to have been mere pawns at the hands of the whimsical and uncaring Squire York (Vol. 2, Chapters 11–14).

Squire York's refusal to move with the times is satirized at various points in the novel through the overblown descriptions of the family silver salt holder (*saleiro*), an heirloom that becomes the material symbol of old privilege. He is so generally hated that, immediately after Joe's trial, his mansion, Durham Hall, is set on fire (Vol. 2, Chapter 14). This is one of the scenes in the novel that attests to social unrest (another being in Vol. 2, Chapter 11, when in the meeting immediately prior to the trial the crowd is described as a living animal, in a way that is reminiscent of a violent clash in *North and South*). Although we never discover who the culprit of the fire might have been, there is an assumption that it is likely to have been one of Leofrico Catecumeno's own workers. But the authoritarian aristocrat remains arrogant and defiant. Just before this setback, which leaves him more isolated than ever before, he had furthermore forbidden Henrique to marry Maria, the daughter of his political rival, Arthur, before reaching his majority, and threatened to disown him if he did. At the receiving end of the disproportionate power of an unwise patriarch, it is not surprising that, by this point, Henrique should choose to side entirely with the Severn family.

Simultaneously, the theme of social climbing is spotlighted through the portrayal of scheming and ruthless Nanny Quemmequer, who is in competition with Maria in a bid to secure Henrique's love and, moreover, social advancement. Although she never succeeds in winning his heart, she eventually manages to separate Henrique from his beloved Maria out of pure spite — rather improbably by printing in *The Times* an announcement of her own wedding to the dashing bachelor. Thus the Austen-like progression towards enlightenment present in the novels of Júlio Dinis is tragically curtailed with the bleak ending of *Maria Severn* as Maria, believing herself to have been betrayed, is first struck by illness, and then goes on to commit suicide by drowning herself in the River Test.

The question is, why does the ending of *Maria Severn* not allow for any easy 'national' reconciliation? Despite a narrative focus on the development of the main protagonists, and just as opposites seem to have reached a degree of reconciliation, Maria's suicide forecloses the possibility of a happy ending. Moreover her cousin, the deserving Jorge, who had been secretly in love with her, is unable to rescue her or provide an alternative happy ending. In so doing, the Portuguese novel may conceivably have taken its cue from a famous article published anonymously in the *Westminster Review* in 1856 entitled 'Silly Novels by Lady Novelists', which Wood may have read or heard about, since she was living in England at the time. If so, she may have taken on board the criticism levelled there at the majority of the commercial novels by women. Its author, none other than George Eliot as it subsequently transpired, objected to their disregard for reality ('silly novels by lady novelists rarely introduce us into any other than very lofty and fashionable society') and their sugar-coated endings ('whatever vicissitudes she may undergo, from being dashed out of her carriage to having her head shaved in a fever, she comes out of them all with a complexion more blooming and locks more redundant than ever').[34] Eliot did however identify three women of genius as her article drew to a close: Harriet Martineau, Charlotte Bronte (referred to as Currer Bell) and Elizabeth Gaskell.[35] Of those, Gaskell in particular seems to have offered a model for delineating the compassionate, as well as a strong-minded, Maria.

It is moreover conceivable that Wood might have come across *The Mill on the Floss*, which Eliot had published in book form in 1860, to critical acclaim. Although Eliot's subject matter is rather different, the beginning and the ending of *Maria Severn* arguably share some similarities with this Victorian masterpiece. In both cases the heroines drown at the end, while both opening chapters deploy the use of a first-person narrator, which then gives way to a frequently omniscient voice in the rest of the novel (though it is still interspersed with occasional 'I' statements). Major differences between the two novels are the constant rejection of Maggie's talents by her family and society, highlighted by a number of critics, which is quite different to Maria's situation within a supportive family. Moreover, Maria's love problems are rather different to Maggie's entanglements, as the former only has one love interest, seemingly building up towards marriage, until the final twist.

In keeping with the argument that she had rehearsed in the *Westminster Review*, George Eliot refused to give a rosy ending to her novels, leading Rohan

---

[34] George Eliot, 'Silly Novels by Lady Novelists' [1856], in *The Westminster Review*, October 1856, pp. 442–61 (p. 443), available online at <http://www.bl.uk/collection-items/silly-novels-by-lady-novelists-essay-by-george-eliot>. Also reprinted in *The Essays of George Eliot* (New York: Funk & Wagnalls, 1883), pp. 178–204 (p. 180; p. 179).

[35] Eliot, 'Silly Novels', *Westminster Review*, p. 460; *Essays*, p. 202.

Maitzen to affirm:

> The ending of *The Mill on the Floss* has been controversial since the novel's first publication. It has been interpreted as both triumphant and tragic, as celebrating both death and love, as calling for revenge or for mourning. Whatever it means, it does not offer the satisfying resolution expected from a bildungsroman. If anything, it defies our wish for satisfaction, along with the novelistic conventions that usually provide it, and thus provokes us to imagine — and maybe even work for — the changes that would have made Maggie's novel of development into the kind of story she wishes for.[36]

Francisca Wood's novel, part novel of manners and part bildungsroman, may seem likewise to have a controversial ending. Insofar as she wished to avoid the satisfying conventional happy ending that she seemed to be gearing up to, *à la* Austen or Gaskell, she had to rely on a *deus ex machina*: the destructive intervention of the evil spurned lover, Nanny. In so doing she too 'defies our wish for satisfaction', but forces us to reflect on the repercussions that any human behaviour, whether good or bad, can have on both individual and, by extension, collective destinies. In other words she too 'provokes us to imagine — and maybe even work for' a better outcome.

In the epilogue of *The Mill on the Floss*, set some years later, Philip, and Stephen and Lucy together, visit Maggie and Tom's grave. This closing scene, too, seems to be echoed in the final paragraphs of *Maria Severn* where, after Maria's untimely suicide, all that seems left to Henrique and Jorge is to mourn their beloved, perpetually. One small consolation is that both male characters carry on with Maria's good deeds, looking after the schools that she had set up in Olston Vale, thereby ensuring that her progressive legacy remains alive. There is ultimately a Christian, philanthropic message to the novel, and this also applies to the punishment meted out to Nanny: rather than having her tried by official justice, which would have resulted in transportation (*degredo*), it is agreed instead that her hair is to be shaved off by Henrique at regular intervals, the equivalent of female castration. In other words, it is because Henrique is denied a happy ending that his moral regeneration is consolidated, leading him to apply relative clemency to Nanny and undertake to make a difference to others in a less fortunate financial position than himself. What is ultimately clear is that Wood, aiming for radical and widespread social change, wished to co-opt men in her ambitious reformist agenda. This may also explain why her work was dedicated to her Portuguese nephew, Clarimundo Martins, whom she addresses at the beginning and the end of the two volumes.[37]

By way of conclusion, one must ask: how could such a readable, progressive and thought-provoking novel disappear from sight? Firstly, as was already

---

[36] Rohan Maitzen, 'The Mill on the Floss as bildungsroman', online at <http://www.bl.uk/romantics-and-victorians/articles/the-mill-on-the-floss-as-bildungsroman>.

[37] According to <http://geneall.net/pt/forum/148786/a-familia-burnay-e-cabo-verde/#a185499>, Clarimundo Martins (1835–1895), married Apolónia Ferreira Martins Burnay, on 15 December 1871. He subsequently moved to Cape Verde, working for Banco Nacional Ultramarino.

pointed out, it is not an isolated instance in respect of nineteenth-century Portuguese women writers. Secondly, *Maria Severn* may have been snubbed as the work of an *estrangeirada*, not least since Wood's lengthy residence in England means that there are *anglicismos* in her work — though they are arguably offset by her fascinating cultural knowledge of Britain (including some hilarious footnotes where she comments on British habits and teaches her readers how to pronounce some words), which makes her a truly transnational writer and commentator. The Portuguese elite, unfamiliar with the British tradition of nineteenth-century women's writing, may have failed to grasp the novelty of this work, and its engagement with Austen, Gaskell and Eliot, which make it such a novel and compelling offering in the context of nineteenth-century Portuguese literature. Ultimately, however, I think the explanation for the lack of attention may lie elsewhere: in *Uma história na História*, Chatarina Edfeldt highlights several mechanisms of exclusion of women from the canon and Wood's work is likely to have fallen foul to one such mechanism in particular, namely the silencing of works that deal with gender inequality and feminist questions.[38]

One decade before Eça de Queirós, Wood sought to ensure the wider circulation of ideas and debates propagated by the Victorian press, in order to instigate progress in her country of birth, something that deserves an in-depth study in its own right. But, quite apart from her role as a potential female mentor and public intellectual, Francisca Wood's progressive agenda means that her pioneer literary efforts simultaneously deserve to be rewritten into the canon. The recovery of *Maria Severn* is urgently needed to re-establish its rightful place in Portuguese cultural memory as part of a tradition that includes two well-known Anglophile writers, namely Júlio Dinis and Eça de Queirós. Since Wood's novel has languished all but unread for nearly 150 years, my aim is to ensure that it is shortly made available in a modern edition. My hope is that it will offer a decisive contribution to the revision of deep-rooted assumptions about the lack of any significant female novelist in nineteenth-century Portugal. For my contention is that Wood, in the footsteps of George Eliot, was able to 'pour in the right elements: genuine observation, humour, and passion' into her literary work.[39]

---

[38] Chatarina Edfeldt, *Uma história na História: representações da autoria feminina na História da Literatura Portuguesa do século XX* (Montijo: Câmara Municipal de Montijo, 2006).
[39] Eliot, 'Silly Novels', *Westminster Review*, p. 461; *Essays*, p. 203.

Undone Anatomies:
Femininity, Performativity and Parody in Mário de Sá-Carneiro's *A Confissão de Lúcio*

ELEANOR K. JONES

University of Manchester

For the modern reader, the disorientating erotic elements of Mário de Sá-Carneiro's 1914 novel *A Confissão de Lúcio* [*Lúcio's Confession*], set in the bohemian milieux of *fin-de-siècle* Lisbon and Paris, are difficult to pass over.[1] Charting the series of events that leads the eponymous narrator first to embark on an affair with Marta, the wife of his best friend Ricardo, and shortly thereafter to attempt to murder her — only to discover that her body has been somehow supplanted by that of Ricardo — the text's relentless intensity and erotic charge serve to foreground the sexual body in a way that makes its pervasive presence and influence undeniable. Until as recently as twenty years ago, however, analyses of the novel were limited to modernist or decadentist readings that acknowledged Sá-Carneiro's use of eroticism but left its complexities overlooked.[2] Attempts to navigate the possibility of homoeroticism in the novel, meanwhile, were all too often concerned with discussing the supposed closeted homosexuality of Sá-Carneiro himself, a sexual–textual assimilation of author and work that Anna M. Klobucka has identified as a persistent trend within Lusophone Studies.[3] The rapid expansion of queer theory in the 1990s, and its gradual entrance into mainstream academic discourse during the 2000s, served to provide and refine the critical tools and discursive space necessary for an exploration into the ways in which gender and sexuality operate in the novel, and more recent readings, most prominently those of Fernando Arenas,

---

[1] Mário de Sá-Carneiro, *A Confissão de Lúcio*, 9th edn (Lisbon: Nova Ática, 1945). Further references will be given in the text as *CL* followed by the page number. English translations are taken from Mário de Sá-Carneiro, *Lúcio's Confession*, trans. by Margaret Jull Costa (Sawtry, Cambridgeshire: Dedalus, 1993).

[2] Mary Elizabeth Ginway, 'Transgendering in Luso-Brazilian Speculative Fiction from Machado de Assis to the Present', *Luso-Brazilian Review*, 47.1 (2010), 40–60 (p. 50).

[3] Anna M. Klobucka, 'Was Camões Gay? Queering the Portuguese Literary Canon', paper delivered at the Annual Convention of the Modern Language Association, 28 December 2007. For examples of this tendency, see Pamela Bacarisse, *A alma amortalhada: Mário de Sá-Carneiro's Use of Metaphor and Image* (London: Tamesis, 1984), and more recently Eduardo Pitta, *Fractura: a condição homossexual na literatura portuguesa contemporânea* (Coimbra: Angelus Novus, 2003).

Ana Luísa Amaral and Cláudia Pazos-Alonso, have made use of this space, identifying sublimated homosexual desire as central to the text's plot and narrative tension.

Such readings have focused primarily on the relationship between narrator Lúcio and protagonists Ricardo and Marta, positing Marta as triangulated within the matrix of Lúcio and Ricardo's repressed mutual desire. For Arenas, this triangulation is the dramatic locus of the novel, with gay desire at once ubiquitous throughout Sá-Carneiro's narrative and altogether absent from it: a paradoxical (non-)presence that is mirrored by the text's shifting portrayal of a homoeroticism that is both deeply repressed and persistently on the brink of exploding into polymorphous sensuality.[4] This destabilization of gendered subjectivities, Arenas affirms, is achieved by means of the novel's consistent problematization of the notion of truth, 'tanto a nível ontológico como ficcional' [on an ontological as well as fictional level].[5] Despite exerting this troubling effect on gender and sexual roles, however, for Arenas the text is nonetheless predicated on the misogynistic objectification of Marta, as she is reduced to nothing more than the means by which Lúcio and Ricardo negotiate and socially sanction their mutual attraction. In this way, Arenas affirms,[6] Sá-Carneiro's characterization of Lúcio and Ricardo's relationship reflects Eve Kosofsky Sedgwick's concept of homosocial desire, which posits female objectification as the primary means by which male–male relations are reified and mediated.[7]

The fluidity of gender and sexual categories that Arenas sees as central to *Confissão*'s subversive potential is a key element of Amaral's argument, which makes use of the contemporary poststructuralist theories of sexuality expounded by Sedgwick and by Judith Butler to elucidate the challenges to sexual normativity posed by Sá-Carneiro's poetry, prose fiction and personal letters. Particularly significant for Amaral is Sá-Carneiro's affinity with the feminine,[8] a self-identification implicitly reflected by the tacitly feminized features of his male characters and poetic personae.[9] For Amaral, this sliding of gendered signifiers works in tandem with the author's strategically ambivalent use of gender stereotypes to expose the performative roots of gender identity, thereby troubling the naturalized status of gender as a whole.[10] These tactical

---

[4] Fernando Arenas, 'Onde existir? A (im)possibilidade excessiva do desejo homoerótico na ficção de Mário de Sá-Carneiro', *Metamorfoses*, 6 (2005), 159–68 (p. 159).
[5] Arenas, p. 163.
[6] Arenas, p. 165.
[7] See Eve Kosofsky Sedgwick, *Between Men: English Literature and Male Homosocial Desire* (Chichester, NY: Columbia University Press, 1985).
[8] Ana Luísa Amaral, '"Durmo o crepúsculo": lendo a poética de Mária de Sá-Carneiro a partir das teorias contemporâneas sobre as sexualidades', in *Subjectividades em devir: estudos de poesia moderna e contemporânea*, ed. by Célia Pedrosa and Ida Alves (Rio de Janeiro: Editora 7Letras, 2008), pp. 9–17 (p. 10).
[9] Amaral, p. 12.
[10] Amaral, p. 12.

reappropriations of binary gender constructs are intertwined, in *Confissão*, with the ambiguous relationship between Lúcio and Ricardo, which Amaral reads as displaying the hallmarks of Butler's concept of gender abjection: those forms of gender expression that are culturally unthinkable and subjectively repellent, and yet continue to menace the subject with their liminal presence, serving as an unpredictable reminder of the fragility of gendered boundaries.[11] In Pazos-Alonso's Freudian analysis, meanwhile, Lúcio's eponymous confession is read as a 'quasi-clinical "document"' in which these unthinkable desires are sublimated via the oneiric devices of displacement and condensation, which serve both to conceal and subtly betray the homoerotic narrative underlying the novel's ostensibly heterosexual central love triangle.[12]

These groundbreaking readings have without a doubt dramatically reframed conventional understandings of Sá-Carneiro's text, opening the door to fresh exploration of the characterization of his male protagonists and the enigmatic relationship between them. His women characters, however, remain excluded from examination as gendered and sexual beings in their own right, leaving a gap in the current critical literature that this study seeks to address. Building on the critical precedents outlined above, particularly that set by Amaral, and making use of Butler's extensively developed poststructuralist understandings of gender performativity, parody and abjection, the study aims to foreground the intricate and complex contributions of the text's two women characters — Marta, and the unnamed woman known only as 'a americana' [the American] — to the novel's radical destabilization of naturalized gender and sexual constructs.

As the first link in the fantastic chain of events that leads ultimately to the disintegration of Lúcio's stable sense of self, the American woman's party represents a sharp turning point in Sá-Carneiro's text. Taking place a short way into the narrative, the party is figured as a dreamlike sequence, and is couched heavily in the opulent language of decadence, excess and eroticism, centred around an abstract stage performance by the American woman herself that Ricardo later dubs the 'Orgia do Fogo' (*CL*, 45) ['Orgy of Fire' (36)]. The framing of the sequence as explicitly transgressive and overtly sexual perhaps explains why otherwise gender-focused studies have stopped short of deconstructing it in gendered terms. Richard Vernon, for example, characterizes the scene as transgressing normative heterosexual codification only in terms of the American woman's ability to control the audience with her beauty, a seizing of power he interprets as her 'usurping of masculinity',[13] while Arenas suggests its synaesthetic blurring of sensory meanings might speak to a broader

---

[11] Amaral, p. 14.
[12] Cláudia Pazos-Alonso, 'Displacement and Condensation: A Freudian Analysis of *A Confissão de Lúcio*', *Journal of Romance Studies*, 11.3 (2011), 65–76 (p. 66).
[13] Richard Vernon, 'Demented Disclosures and the Art of Seeing in *A Confissão de Lúcio*', *Hispanófila*, 146 (2006), 37–48 (p. 42).

destabilization of naturalized categories.[14] Despite their shared recognition of the scene's subversive potential, however, neither study fully untangles the essential means by which the American woman incites this gendered disruption. The question remains: how exactly does Sá-Carneiro's depiction of the American woman and her performance act as the spark for the dramatic explosion of gender categories that ensues?

The American woman, referred to in the original text only as 'a americana' [the American], 'a mulher fulva' (*CL*, 33) ['the flame-haired woman' (27)], or variations thereof, remains anonymous throughout Lúcio's two brief but significant encounters with her. Her early identification as a lesbian, 'uma grande sáfica' (*CL*, 33) ['a follower of Sappho' (27)], is the only inner attribute Sá-Carneiro discloses to the reader; beyond that, his writing of her character is limited to tangible physical features, divesting her of personal narrative or subjective backstory. This singular emphasis on the corporeal is furthered by Lúcio's repeated narrative references to fetishized body parts, particularly her bare feet and gold-painted toenails (*CL*, 30–43). Her sexually charged performance of an unfamiliar abstract dance is made all the more striking by her physical appearance and dress, both somewhat anachronistic and exotic in the novel's nineteenth-century European setting. Her tight metallic tunic reveals a nipple, her hair is full of jewels, and, as Pamela Bacarisse notes, there is specific narrative attention paid to painted body parts:[15] as she strips, she reveals that her breasts and vulva, like her lips and toenails, are painted gold (*CL*, 44). The two dancers that join her onstage, their bodies at once muscle-bound, curvaceous and painted with flowers, arouse unsettling sexual urges in the male audience members; the masculine appearance of one dancer's legs in particular provoke in Lúcio 'desejos brutais de as morder' (*CL*, 41) ['the violent urge to bite them' (33)].

The American woman's transparent embodiment of a corporeality specifically coded as female, illustrated by her breasts, vulva, painted lips and nails, and long embellished hair, frames her performance as manifesting an excessive hyperfemininity, a modality that can be located on Butler's schema of gender parody. In her comprehensive deconstruction of gendered meanings and identities, Butler redefines gender not as a 'being', but as a 'doing', a 'stylized repetition of acts' that 'constitute the illusion of an abiding gendered self' and are symbiotically circumscribed, controlled and sustained by the maintenance of a strictly enforced system of compulsory heterosexuality.[16] Gender is not consciously espoused by a prediscursive agent: on the contrary, Butler's framework precludes the possibility of a pre-gendered subject. Rather, it posits gender as ultimately performative, in that its existence as a fundamental marker

---

[14] Arenas, p. 163.
[15] Bacarisse, p. 6.
[16] Judith Butler, *Gender Trouble* (London: Routledge, 2007), pp. 191–93.

of identity is constituted through its continual realization.[17] It is by means of this repeated enactment that gender materializes, *'stabiliz[ing] over time to produce the effect of boundary, fixity, and surface'*,[18] while nonetheless remaining 'a complexity whose totality is permanently deferred, never fully what it is at any given juncture in time'.[19] The very necessity of repeated affirmation can thus expose this ephemeral and contingent quality, revealing and expanding the 'gaps and fissures' in the naturalized illusion societally recognized as gender identity.[20]

This initial premise acts as the starting point for Butler's inquiry into forms of repetition or reiteration that have the potential to destabilize gender constructs, rather than reproducing and consolidating them. She proposes two gendered modalities that present such possibilities, both figured as forms of 'gender parody': drag performance, and lesbian butch and femme aesthetics.[21] Drag, by achieving its entertainment value through the hyperbolic displacement of the relationship between perceived anatomy, gender identity and performed gender, brings into relief the dissonances and disparities between these categories; furthermore, as a conscious and literal performance of gender, it underscores the performativity at the heart of gender identities as a whole.[22] Butch and femme lesbian identities and aesthetics, meanwhile, appear superficially to replicate heterosexual constructs while ultimately refusing heterosexual desire, thus revealing the 'utterly constructed status of the so-called heterosexual original'.[23] In other words, such modalities parody ostensibly 'original' genders in a way that troubles the very notion of originality.[24]

Elements of both these 'disordering practices' can be seen at play in the American woman's performance, highlighting her role as an antagonist of gendered structures in the text and contributing to the scene's unsettling qualities.[25] The sensuality and eroticism of the performance suggest a courting of male heterosexual desire, and hegemonic concepts of the enforced relationship between gender identity and sexual desire dictate therefore that this flamboyant display of overtly sexual hyperfemininity should work to reinforce the heterosexual matrix and the oppositional constitution of masculinity. The assumed provocation of heterosexual desire by means of feminine display, however, is ultimately displaced by the American woman's lesbian identification, and by her dancers' masculine excess of muscle. Like the femme aesthetics explored in Butler's work, then, the American woman's performance comes

---

[17] Butler, *Gender Trouble*, p. 34.
[18] Judith Butler, *Bodies that Matter* (London: Routledge, 2007), p. xviii. All quoted italics are present in original texts.
[19] Butler, *Gender Trouble*, p. 22.
[20] Butler, *Bodies that Matter*, p. xix.
[21] Butler, *Gender Trouble*, p. 187.
[22] Butler, *Gender Trouble*, pp. 186–88.
[23] Butler, *Gender Trouble*, p. 43.
[24] Butler, *Gender Trouble*, p. 168.
[25] Butler, *Gender Trouble*, p. 24.

instead to enact a sudden rupture in the dominant framework of compulsory heterosexuality: a deliberate stoppage in the continuity between perceived gender identity and sexual object choice that upholds the cultural intelligibility of gendered categories.[26]

Alongside an interruption of compulsory heterosexuality brought about by the slippage between assigned gender and sexual practice, the American woman's performance troubles the association between anatomy and performed gender that forms a further axis of the gender matrix as theorized by Butler. In this way, the American woman can be seen as engaging in a Butlerian understanding of drag performance. While traditional drag artists achieve a sense of gendered dissonance by staging and playing with the incongruence between anatomy and performed gender, literally performing genders in exaggerated opposition to those societally assigned to them, the American woman achieves the same valuable disparity by espousing a version of femininity that so exceeds dominant demarcations of 'the feminine' that it is itself incompatible with female-coded anatomy. Through a staged performance of her assigned gender that goes so far as to render itself discursively unrecognizable, a status manifest in the attendees' difficulties in articulating what they have witnessed (*CL*, 45–46), the American woman pushes at the boundaries of binary gender in the novel, threatening the assumed impermeability of its internal split and irreversibly disturbing the coherence of the other characters' hitherto stable gender identities. Lúcio's growing aversion to her sexed body, reaching a visceral peak with his description of her genitalia as a 'terrível flor de carne a estrebuchar agonias magentas' (*CL*, 44) ['terrible flower of flesh moving in convulsive magenta spasms' (35)], confirms the troubling influence of her monstrously excessive gender performance. His reaction, affective, uncontrollable and confused, here anticipates the fundamental sense of personal and interpersonal disruption that come to dominate the protagonists' narratives following the orgiastic scenes at the American woman's party.

If the American woman's party can be seen as the catalyst for the chain reaction that ultimately results in the explosion of fixed gender categories in the novel's denouement, the character of Marta represents a further incendiary element. As the wife of Ricardo, Marta is initially presented as a flesh-and-blood character, a 'linda mulher loira, muito loira, alta, escultural' (*CL*, 78) ['a beautiful woman, very blonde, tall and statuesque' (61)] with a 'rosto formosíssimo, de uma beleza vigorosa, talhado em oiro' (*CL*, 78) ['[a face that] was truly lovely, it had a vigorous beauty, as if carved out of gold' (61)]. Following a tumultuous sexual affair with Lúcio, however, she is revealed to be nothing more than Ricardo's phantasmic creation, his 'fantástico Mistério' (*CL*, 157) ['fantastic Mystery' (115)] that vanishes before Lúcio's eyes 'como se extingue uma chama' when he fires his gun at her (*CL*, 157) ['like a flame being extinguished' (115)]. Past critical readings of Marta have defined her as the conduit for Ricardo and

---

[26] Butler, *Gender Trouble*, p. 24.

Lúcio's closeted mutual desire, the necessary third point of their homosocial triangulation.²⁷ For Arenas, Marta is a chimera through which the male protagonists strengthen this homosocial bond, resolving homoerotic desires while precluding the emergence of gay panic or the disruption of sexual categories.²⁸ Pazos-Alonso, in a similar vein, sees her in Freudian terms as a 'dream vision, into which socially prohibited desires can be channelled in a more acceptable form'.²⁹ Both critics thus read Marta as an ephemeral being who stabilizes sexual and gender identities in the novel by resolving the threat to compulsory heterosexuality posed by the sexual tension between Ricardo and Lúcio. Further deconstruction of Marta's specific attributes as a figure of fantasy, however, can in fact produce an alternative reading, recasting her as destabilizing hegemonic gender categories through her very embodiment of objectified femininity.

Even prior to Marta's appearance as his fantastic creation, Ricardo's imagining of womanhood fits squarely into the concept of femininity outlined by Butler as merely a set of 'acts and gestures, articulated and enacted desires [that] create the illusion of an interior and organising gender core, an illusion discursively maintained for the regulation of sexuality within the obligatory framework of reproductive heterosexuality'.³⁰ In a revealing conversation with Lúcio early in the text, he confirms that the element of femininity most attractive to him is not beauty, but 'outra coisa mais vaga — imponderável, translúcida: *a gentileza*' (*CL*, 65) ['something vaguer than that, something imponderable, translucent: *kindness*' (51)], an attribute that arouses within him '*uma ânsia sexual* de possuir' (65) ['a *sexual longing* to possess' (51)]. Ricardo's verbal display of a singular and intense attraction to the element of femininity that he appears to perceive as encouraging the exertion of male sexual dominance exemplifies his mental reduction of femininity to those performative aspects that work to consolidate hegemonic masculinity and thereby to confirm men's superior position in the hierarchy of gender. This implied affinity with hegemonic masculinity, however, is troubled by Ricardo's frequent corporeal identification with those same excessively submissive feminine traits; Lúcio describes a conversation with his friend in which he expresses his envy of 'uma mulher admirável, estiraçada sobre um leito de rendas; olhando a sua carne toda nua... esplêndida...' (*CL*, 68–69) ['a lovely woman, stretched out on a coverlet of lace, contemplating her own naked flesh... splendid' (54)], before putting himself in her place, filled with 'um desejo perdido de ser mulher' (*CL*, 69) ['a mad desire to be a woman' (54)]. Implicit within this juxtaposition of sexual attraction to exaggerated female submission and a secretive, quasi-autoerotic identification with it is the heavy presence of masculine crisis, a menacing fissure in Ricardo's

---

²⁷ See Bacarisse, p. 8; Arenas, pp. 164–66; Pazos-Alonso, p. 70.
²⁸ Arenas, pp. 164–66.
²⁹ Pazos-Alonso, p. 70.
³⁰ Butler, *Gender Trouble*, pp. 185–86.

sense of gendered internal coherence that can only be affectively resolved through an equally exaggerated performance of masculine domination. On this schema, Marta becomes the intended object of that performance, the submissive surface upon which Ricardo can steady his sense of self.

When Marta is examined in light of her status as Ricardo's creation, this role as hypersubmissive object seems increasingly to define her as a character. In Lúcio's narration of his first encounter with her, he mentions that her hands are so slender and pale — implicitly weak — that they are 'inquietantes' (*CL*, 78) ['disquiet[ing]' (61)]. In spite of displaying 'uma finíssima inteligência' (*CL*, 79) ['a sharp intellect' (62)], she has no opinions or ideas of her own, merely mirroring those of Ricardo; neither, it transpires, does she appear to have any memories (*CL*, 79–84). This inexplicable lack of narrative or independent personality acquires a more fantastic and horrifying gloss when Lúcio witnesses her visibly fading out in front of his eyes, her very physicality disintegrating 'até que desapareceu por completo' (*CL*, 87) ['until she had disappeared completely' (67)]. During their affair, Lúcio begins to experience the disturbing and uncanny sensation that Marta does not exist when he is not with her (*CL*, 108). Later, as the novel's grip on the fabric of reality loosens, Lúcio discovers Marta's infidelity with their mutual acquaintance Sérgio Warginsky, and bites her breast in rage. He bruises and breaks her skin until he tastes blood, but Marta does not cry out, pull away, or even appear to 'notar essa carícia brutal' (*CL*, 124) ['to notice that brutal caress' (92)].

Marta's unstable corporeality, her lack of personal narrative, and her unwavering adherence to Ricardo's desires suggest that rather than the autonomous 'being' she appears, she can instead be defined as a specifically gendered 'doing': her ephemeral 'existence' is constituted exclusively by her performance of femininity, one that seeks only to confirm and uphold compulsory heterosexuality through the courting of masculine desire. She is a fantasy figure reduced purely to gendered performance, created to resolve Ricardo's sexually dysphoric crisis, and thus lacks any appearance of subjective interiority. But rather than contributing to any successful reinforcement of heterosexual desire or the gendered categories it entails, this very failure to maintain the appearance of a cohesive interior selfhood is what renders her an ultimately destabilizing presence. Her transparent lack of interior essence, of any illusion of substance, only troubles the foundations of selfhood in the novel, showing the notion itself of an abiding gendered interiority to be nothing more than a fictive construct.

Lúcio's references to an indefinable feeling of unease or instability, which increase in both frequency and intensity as the novel progresses, provide evidence of this interpretation of Marta, reflecting the mounting pressure her presence exerts on his internal stability. After their first meeting, Lúcio feels himself to have been in 'um mundo de sonhos' (*CL*, 77) ['a world of dreams' (60)], and later, on recalling their illicit sexual activity, he is hit by 'incompreensíveis náuseas'

(*CL*, 105) ['an incomprehensible feeling of nausea' (80)]. As the novel progresses, this vague unease is supplanted by a near-constant state of internal torture (*CL*, 115). Ricardo's sense of self is likewise gradually destroyed by Marta's presence, a slow disintegration that manifests physically when he looks into a mirror and cannot see his own reflection (*CL*, 100). Finally, as the novel closes, each man is revealed to have lost his subject status: Lúcio is incarcerated by the state and thus divested of autonomy indefinitely, and Ricardo dies, mysteriously, at the precise moment that he shoots Marta and she vanishes (*CL*, 157–58).

Sá-Carneiro's writing of both the American woman and Marta can thus be seen to destabilize fixed gender and sexual categories in the novel by bringing the fundamental performativity of all genders into relief. While both characters ultimately realize these subversive ends, however, their means are highly divergent, with the American woman's staged performance of an excessive femininity contrasting sharply with Marta's reduction to a set of meticulously reiterated and idealized feminine acts. The apparent paradox at play in the seemingly symmetrical eventualities of these two very different women becomes more coherent when the characters are understood as occupying the novel's sphere of gendered abjection. Appropriating Julia Kristeva's theory of the abject as at once within the subject and necessarily disavowed to maintain the subject's ongoing integrity, Butler demonstrates that key to the continuity of the gender binary is the production of an adjacent domain of abject, unintelligible bodies, wherein reside those 'gendered beings who appear to be persons but who fail to conform to the gendered norms of cultural intelligibility by which persons are defined'.[31] While the emergence of the gendered subject relies on the repudiation of the abject, however, the abject sphere continues to trouble the subject, presenting a persistent threat of disruption and destabilization to the subject's base integrity. In order to maintain his or her sense of internal stability, the subject must therefore repeatedly disavow the abject realm; in turn, it is because of this need for perpetual disavowal that the abject takes on a mercurial changeability, perpetually unmade and redefined.[32]

Lúcio's narrative treatment of the American woman and Marta clearly points to the location of both characters within the novel's abject sphere. The refusal of Lúcio and his companions to discuss the American woman or her party beyond their conversation immediately after the event (*CL*, 46) indicates a tacit collective agreement to exclude her from the domain of the thinkable, rendering her abject, in order to resolve the threat to their individual subjectivities posed by her subversion of gendered and sexual norms. Lúcio's growing sensations of unease, repulsion and finally agony during his affair with Marta can likewise be understood as resulting from his growing efforts to fix her position in the abject realm, continually reinscribing a boundary that by its very definition is fundamentally permeable and thus readily transgressed. The marking of

---

[31] Butler, *Gender Trouble*, p. 23.
[32] Butler, *Gender Trouble*, pp. 181–82.

both women characters with this abject status despite their clear differences further posits their exclusion from the subjective sphere as part of Lúcio's increasingly desperate efforts to stabilize his sense of gendered self through the consolidation of internal coherence and disavowal of troubling elements. Significantly, however, this obsessive attempt to stabilize and restabilize selfhood by repeatedly circumscribing the boundary between subject and abject is ultimately revealed as futile, resulting only in Lúcio's exclusion from the subjective domain. Over the course of Lúcio's narrative, then, the very notion of the stable gendered self becomes radically problematized, as the coherence, integrity and stability of each character, including the narrator himself, is called into question.

The application of Butler's understandings of sex and gender to Sá-Carneiro's novel creates a starting point for the development of a new perspective on the ways that the author utilizes gender and sexuality, providing the potential for queer readings that challenge critical assumptions not only of the text's representation and use of heterosexuality, but also of its subscription to any fixed categories of gender and sex. With this study, I have sought to expand on one such reading, highlighting the importance of the American woman to the text's gender narrative while challenging the interpretation of Marta as a stabilizing presence by redefining her as a source of gender trouble. *A Confissão de Lúcio* is ultimately shown to expose the fragility and contingency of gender constructs, making complex use of performativity and parody to demonstrate the means by which gender can be recast, as Butler would have it, as 'thoroughly and radically *incredible*'.[33]

---

[33] Butler, *Gender Trouble*, p. 193.

'A fabulous speck on the Earth's surface': Depictions of Colonial Macao in 1950s' Hollywood

RUI LOPES

Universidade Nova, Lisbon

European colonialism was in the background, and even forefront, of several North American fiction films, including classics such as *Gunga Din* (1939) and *Casablanca* (1942).[1] The Portuguese empire had its own share of screen time, particularly in the case of the Asian colony of Macao, which was featured in over a dozen Hollywood productions while under Portuguese rule. With a population of 250,000–300,000 Chinese (around 95% of its entire citizenry) and a continually expanding tourism industry, reaching over 1,250,000 tourists a year by the late 1960s, Macao was a peculiar colony in the context of the Portuguese empire, and one that gained a disproportionate projection.[2]

While motion pictures can provide diverse insights into the ways in which the largest film industry in the Western world engaged with Macao, this analysis will focus on their implications in terms of presenting Portuguese colonial rule. The article will begin by contextualizing the general patterns of Macao's screen presence, particularly in the 1950s, when there was a significant spike in American productions set in this colony. Taking into account the different scales of distribution and mass appeal, special attention will be given to films that brought greater visibility to Macao. We will therefore zoom in on the three highest profile productions of that era to feature the Portuguese colony, both as a central and as a peripheral — and contrasting — location in Hong Kong-set political dramas. The article examines how the articulation between, on the one hand, Macao's historical and geographical characteristics, and, on the other, Hollywood's orientalist conventions and hyperbolic sense of spectacle ended up conjuring an overall image of 'subaltern colonialism'.

---

[1] *Gunga Din*, Dir. George Stevens, RKO Radio Pictures, 1942; *Casablanca*, Dir. Michael Curtiz, Warner Bros, 1942. For a brief look at film fiction's early engagement with colonialism, see James Burns, 'Cinema', in *Colonialism: An International, Social, Cultural, and Political Encyclopedia*, 3 vols, ed. by Melvin E. Page and Penny M. Sonnenburg (Santa Barbara, CA: ABC-CLIO, 2003), I, 119–21.

[2] 'Adventure Still Rules Macao; Gals Serve Your Opium at Hotel Bedside', *Variety*, 11 August 1954, p. 2; '5 Casinos Lure Tourists to Macao, Portugal's Beachless, Orient "Resort"', *Variety*, 19 November 1969, p. 2. For a history of Portuguese rule in Macao from the 1930s to the 1970s (during which period the films addressed in this article were released), see Geoffrey Gunn, *Encountering Macau: A Portuguese City-state on the Periphery of China, 1557–1999* (Boulder, CO: Westview, 1996), pp. 95–170; Wu Zhiliang, *Segredos da sobrevivência: história política de Macau* (Macao: Associação de Educação de Adultos de Macau, 1999), pp. 297–374.

Basing his argument on Portugal's 'intermediate economic development' and its mediating position between the centre and the periphery of the modern capitalist system, sociologist Boaventura de Sousa Santos has repeatedly described Portugal as a semi-peripheral country that, by implication, produced a form of semi-peripheral colonialism. According to Santos, since Portugal was itself highly dependent on the core powers of the global political economy, Portuguese society combined traces of both colonizer and colonized, its identity a hybrid between the Shakespearean symbols of the colonial master, Prospero, and the colonized savage, Caliban. The Portuguese empire was then simultaneously shaped by 'a deficit of colonization' (due to Portugal's 'incapacity to colonize efficiently') and by 'an excess of colonization' (with the colonies submitted to a double colonization — by Portugal and, indirectly, by the countries on which Portugal was dependent). Conceptualizing this specificity in relation to the norm of British colonial rule (i.e. the prototype of 'hegemonic colonialism'), Santos recodifies the Portuguese case as subaltern colonialism.[3] In turn, critics have accused such an interpretation of perpetuating a narrative of exceptionality whose lineage includes not only a strand of anti-colonialist critique (Perry Anderson's concept of Portuguese 'ultracolonialism') but also the colonialist justifications employed by the Estado Novo dictatorship (the theory of 'luso-tropicalism', which assigned to the Portuguese empire a high degree of originality and racial harmony).[4] The aim of this article is not to assess the validity of Santos' theses on the ground, but to demonstrate their alignment with the discourse of American film fiction. It will thus contribute to the wider study of the international image of Portugal's empire and the evolving discourse about its colonialism.

During Portuguese rule, Macao consistently remained by far the most visible area of Portugal's empire in North American cinematic fiction. This colony was a primary setting in the thrillers *Smuggler's Island* (1951), *Macao* (1952), *Forbidden* (1953), *Flight to Hong Kong* (1956) and *Hong Kong Confidential* (1958).[5] It served as the location for key scenes in the crime and adventure films

---

[3] Boaventura de Sousa Santos, 'Between Prospero and Caliban: Colonialism, Postcolonialism, and Inter-Identity', *Luso-Brazilian Review*, 39.2 (2002), 9–43. The quoted expressions are taken from pp. 9–11.
[4] Perry Anderson justified the concept of ultracolonialism in a trio of articles titled 'Portugal and the End of Ultra-Colonialism', first published in 1962, in *New Left Review*, first series, issues 15–17. Luso-tropicalism was initially developed by Brazilian sociologist Gilberto Freyre and it was gradually adopted by the Estado Novo dictatorship in the 1950s, as outlined in Cláudia Castelo, *'O modo português de estar no mundo': o luso-tropicalismo e a ideologia colonial portuguesa (1933–1961)* (Porto: Edições Afrontamento, 1998). For a critical assessment of Santos' ideas, see João Leal, *Etnografias portuguesas (1870–1970): cultura popular e identidade nacional* (Lisbon: Publicações Dom Quixote, 2000), pp. 101–03, as well as Eric-Morier Genoud and Michel Cahen, 'Introduction: Portugal, Empire, and Migrations: Was There Ever an Autonomous Imperial Space?', in *Imperial Migrations: Colonial Communities and Diaspora in the Portuguese World*, ed. by Eric-Morier Genoud and Michel Cahen (Basingstoke: Palgrave Macmillan, 2013), pp. 1–28 (pp. 2–7).
[5] *Smuggler's Island*, Dir. Edward Ludwig, Universal Pictures, 1951; *Macao*, Dir. Josef von Sternberg and Nicholas Ray, RKO Pictures, 1952; *Forbidden*, Dir. Rudolph Maté, Universal Pictures, 1953; *Flight to Hong Kong*, Dir. Joseph M. Newman, United Artists, 1956; *Hong Kong Confidential*, Dir. Edward L. Cahn, United Artists, 1958.

Hong Kong Nights (1935), *Dragon's Gold* (1953), *Soldier of Fortune* (1955), *The Scavengers* (1959) and *Cleopatra Jones and the Casino of Gold* (1975), while also playing a smaller role in the plots of *Windjammer* (1937), *Kill a Dragon* (1967) and *That Man Bolt* (1973).[6] Furthermore, Macao was featured in films of other genres, namely the romantic melodrama *Love is a Many-Splendored Thing* (1955) and the social drama *Out of the Tiger's Mouth* (1962).[7] By contrast, other Portuguese colonies were virtually absent from Hollywood's output at the time, with the small exception of the African-based adventure stories *Rope of Sand* (1949), which was mostly set in South Africa yet featured a sequence in a bar in Angola, and *Elephant Stampede* (1951), an entry into the 'Bomba the Jungle Boy' series, which featured two ivory poachers in Africa on their way to unspecified Portuguese territory.[8]

To a great degree, Macao's relative prominence drew on the colony's aura of mystery and adventure, which had already been popularized over the centuries through countless tales of piracy, gambling, espionage, addiction, murder and contraband.[9] Anglophone literature had combined these motifs with descriptions of the colony as a languid, romantic intersection of Western and Eastern cultures, marked by miscegenation and picturesque yet decadent architecture.[10] In the 1930s, the vivid impression of a place of extremes had been notably reinforced by Hendrik de Leeuw's *Cities of Sin*, a mix of travel narrative and investigative report on prostitution and white slavery in Asia, which included the oft-quoted passage:

> There is no question that [Macao] harbors in its hidden places the riffraff of the world, the drunken ship masters, the flotsam of the sea, the derelicts, and more shameless, beautiful, savage women than any port in the world. It is a hell. But to those who whirl in its unending play, it is one haven where

[6] *Hong Kong Nights*, Dir. E. Mason Hopper, distributed by state rights system, 1935; *Dragon's Gold*, Dir. Aubrey Wisberg, United Artists, 1953; *Soldier of Fortune*, Dir. Edward Dmytryk, 20th Century Fox, 1955; *The Scavengers*, Dir. John Cromwell, Hal Roach Distributing Corp. and Valiant Films, 1959; *Cleopatra Jones and the Casino of Gold*, Dir. Charles Bail, Warner Bros., 1975; *Windjammer*, Dir. Ewing Scott, RKO Radio Pictures, 1937; *Kill a Dragon*, Dir. Michael D. Moore, United Artists, 1967; *That Man Bolt*, Dir. David Lowell Rich and Henry Levin, Universal Pictures, 1973. I was unable to locate *Dragon's Gold*, so the analysis is based on the dialogue continuity script available at the British Film Institute (SCR-7134) and on this movie's entry in the American Film Institute [AFI] Catalog of Feature Films <http://www.afi.com/members/catalog/DetailView.aspx?s=&Movie=51188> [accessed 28 September 2014].
[7] *Love Is a Many-Splendored Thing*, Dir. Henry King, 20th Century Fox, 1955; *Out of the Tiger's Mouth*, Dir. Tim Whelan Jr, Path-America Distributing Co. and Astor Pictures, 1962.
[8] *Rope of Sand*, Dir. William Dieterle, Paramount Pictures, 1949; *Elephant Stampede*, Dir. Ford Beebe, Monogram Pictures, 1951. I was unable to locate *Elephant Stampede*, so data is based on the shooting script, available at Wisconsin Center for Film and Theater Research, Walter Mirisch Papers, Box 10, Folder 3.
[9] For a collection of stories, chronicles and poems harking back to the seventeenth century, see *Macao: Mysterious Decay and Romance: An Anthology*, ed. by Donald Pittis and Susan J. Henders (New York: Oxford University Press, 1997).
[10] Rogério Miguel Puga, *A World of Euphemism: Representações de Macau na obra de Austin Coates: 'City of Broken Promises' enquanto romance histórico e bildungsroman feminino* (Lisbon: Fundação Calouste Gulbenkian/Fundação para a Ciência e Tecnologia, 2009), pp. 144–64.

there is never a hand raised or a word said against the play of the beastliest emotions that ever blackened the human heart.[11]

The spike of Macao's popularity in 1950s' cinema can be explained by geographical as well as historical reasons. For Hollywood executives, the economic recovery of Southeast Asia had generated interest in that region's expanding market since the early 1950s,[12] in contrast to less economically developed sub-Saharan Africa, where most other Portuguese colonies were situated.[13] Moreover, as soon as the Korean War (1950-53) broke out — pitting South Korean forces and a US-led United Nations mission against Soviet-backed North Korea, later joined by China — major studios rushed to capitalize on the public's newfound interest in Asian affairs.[14] Macao benefitted from its location on the 'Bamboo Curtain', directly bordering communist China and just a four-hour ferry ride from the British colony of Hong Kong, which made it an ideal setting for plots of Cold War espionage.[15]

Macao also appealed to screenwriters due to particular side effects of Portuguese rule. Because Portugal did not ratify the Bretton Woods monetary agreement until 1961, it was not bound by the same exchange rate for gold as most other countries.[16] According to a famous report in *Life* magazine in 1949, this gave rise to a booming gold trade in Macao, capitalizing on China's craving for gold through smuggling networks between the two territories, which in turn encouraged local piracy.[17] Additionally, from the communist victory in China up to the early 1960s, the Portuguese colony was the only place in the region where open gambling was permitted.[18] All these elements allowed

[11] Hendrik de Leeuw, *Cities of Sin* (New York: Garland Pub, 1979 [1933]), pp. 146-47.
[12] 'Mono Foreign Prexy Sees Better Biz in Asia Than in Europe', *Variety*, 6 March 1950, pp. 1, 10; 'Asia Is Hardly Scratched — Ugast', *Variety*, 24 February 1954, pp. 3, 24.
[13] Pointing out several obstacles and limitations of the African market in the mid-1960s, film critic Robert J. Landry argued that 'As regards motion pictures, and so much else, Africa is "new territory," its story one of development to come rather than development to date.' — 'Africa: Future Film Frontier', *Variety*, 4 May 1966, p. 160.
[14] 'H'wood Scurries To Capitalize On Korean Shooting', *Variety*, 5 July 1950, pp. 3, 22. For an overview of the Korean War, see William Stueck, 'The Korean War', in *Cambridge History of the Cold War, Volume 1: Origins*, ed. by Melvyn P. Leffler and Odd Arne Westad (Cambridge: Cambridge University Press, 2010), pp. 266-87.
[15] 'Adventure Still Rules Macao; Gals Serve Your Opium at Hotel Bedside', *Variety*, 11 August 1954, p. 2. For the significance of Macao in the Cold War during this period, see Michael Share, *Where Empires Collided: Russian and Soviet Relations with Hong Kong, Taiwan, and Macao* (Hong Kong: Chinese University Press, 2007), pp. 242-46.
[16] Michael D. Bordo and Fernando Teixeira dos Santos, 'Portugal and the Bretton Woods International Monetary System', in *International Monetary Systems in Historical Perspective*, ed. by Jaime Reis (Basingstoke: Palgrave Macmillan, 1995), pp. 181-90.
[17] 'Smuggling junks sail with golden cargoes from Macao's cellars', *Life*, 8 August 1949, pp. 22-23. Ten years later, popular British author Ian Fleming explored in greater depth the triads associated with the Macao gold trade in his travelogue *Thrilling Cities* (London: Vintage Books, 2013 [1963]), pp. 25-49. (An excerpt from this text is collected in Pittis and Henders, pp. 61-66.)
[18] 'Korea Paying Satch 30G Weekly to Lift Lid off Orient Version of Las Vegas', *Variety*, 17 January 1963, p. 14. For the evolution of Macao's gambling culture and casino franchise in the colonial era, see António Pinho, 'Gambling in Macau', in *Macau: City of Commerce and Culture*, ed. by Rolf Dieter Cremer (Hong Kong: UEA Press, 1987), pp. 155-64 (pp. 155-58); Sonny Shiu-Hing Lo, *Political*

for distinctive story possibilities, ranging from the pulpy spy twists of *Hong Kong Confidential* to the serious exposé approach of the Golden Berlin Bear-nominated *Out of the Tiger's Mouth*, and even an aborted project for a Macao-based *Casablanca* remake.[19] Repeated exposure then turned this colony into an instantly recognizable backdrop of foreign intrigue.[20]

If its casinos and frontier status made Macao cinematographically attractive, they also meant that films set there tended to emphasize elements of crime and vice. With the exception of the mainstream drama *Love Is a Many-Splendored Thing*, every film contained references to racketeering and most featured gambling and sordid nightclubs. Although Portuguese rule at the time was indeed marked by a mutually beneficial relationship between corrupt colonial bureaucrats and the casino capitalists, including a degree of organized crime,[21] Hollywood helped give Macao's already lurid connotation larger-than-life proportions. A brief dialogue exchange in the otherwise unrelated *The Lady from Shanghai* (1947) had famously identified Macao as the 'wickedest city' in the world.[22] A character explicitly calls back to this line in *Flight to Hong Kong*, before asking the protagonist, Tony Dumont, if Macao really is wicked. Tony replies: 'Well, let's put it this way, in Hong Kong you could get your hair cut, and in Macao you could get your throat cut. The only difference is that in Macao there's no charge.'[23] The tendency to exaggerate was acknowledged by some film critics. Kay Proctor, at the *Los Angeles Examiner*, commented that although 'Macao long has been glamourized in fiction as "the wickedest place on earth"', in fact 'a tourist is perfectly safe trying to win a couple of bucks in the Central Casino playing fan-tan'.[24] Howard McClay, at the *L. A. Daily News*, noted that, aside from illegal dealings and an admittedly thriving gambling industry, the colony's economy also consisted of a prosaic trade in rice, fish, firecrackers, vegetable oil and metal products, but it was not the legitimate end of Macao's business that interested filmmakers.[25]

In American cinema, the colony became particularly associated with smuggling. In the 1930s, the implicit background of the Chinese Civil War had favoured stories about arms contraband to China: in *Hong Kong Nights*, US secret agent Tom Keene tails a gunrunner to Macao; in *Windjammer*, the passengers

Change in Macao (New York: Routledge, 2008), pp. 84–86; Zhidong Hao, *Macau: History and Society* (Hong Kong: Hong Kong University Press, 2011), pp. 73–74; Victor Zheng and Po-san Wan, *Gambling Dynamism: The Macao Miracle* (Heidelberg/New York/Dordrecht/London: Springer-Verlag Berlin Heidelberg, 2014), pp. 32–46.

[19] 'Palm Springs Ripples', *Variety*, 9 March 1961, p. 8.
[20] This may explain, for example, the choice to open *That Man Bolt* in a Macao prison, a detail that is irrelevant to the plot yet allows for some atmospheric establishing shots before the credits.
[21] Lo Shiu Hing, *Political Development in Macao* (Hong Kong: Chinese University Press, 1995), pp. 176–79.
[22] *The Lady from Shanghai*, Dir. Orson Welles, Columbia Pictures, 1947, 04:02–10.
[23] *Flight to Hong Kong*, 06:27–54.
[24] Margaret Herrick Library at the Academy of Motion Pictures Arts and Sciences (AMPAS), General Collection, Forbidden, 'Action Fast in "Forbidden"', *Los Angeles Examiner*, 7 January 1954.
[25] AMPAS, General Collection, Macao, 'Film Review', *L. A. Daily News*, 3 May 1952.

of a shipwrecked yacht are rescued by Captain Morgan, who is carrying out an illegal shipment of guns and ammunitions to the colony. Following *Life* magazine's exposé, in the 1950s the focus shifted to the contraband of gold and jewellery. *Smuggler's Island* concerns the Macao-based, ex-US Navy diver Steve Kent, who is persuaded by his love interest to retrieve gold bars from a crashed airplane and smuggle them into Hong Kong. In *Dragon's Gold*, investigator Mack Rossiter tracks down the employee of a New York bonding company who has apparently absconded with seven million dollars in gold bullions entrusted to him by a Chinese warlord living in the Portuguese colony. *Flight to Hong Kong* follows Macao-based mob operative Tony Dumont, who goes rogue during a diamond smuggling job. In *Hong Kong Confidential*, American intelligence agent Casey Reed worms his way into Macao's underworld by proposing an elaborate scheme to smuggle gold into China. Furthermore, *The Scavengers* contains subplots about the circulation of bonds and narcotics (as implied by the protagonist's cocaine-addicted wife).

Later films would go on to address various kinds of contraband. *Out of the Tiger's Mouth* addresses human traffic in the story of two Chinese orphans who escape from mainland China and seek to reach Hong Kong: the five-year-old girl and the nine-year-old boy are smuggled into Macao and sold to a brothel where they are forced to work as helpers and thieves. In *Kill a Dragon*, the villain is a Portuguese gangster from 'the Mafia of Macao',[26] seeking to retrieve a cargo of nitroglycerine in order to sell it in the black market. The traffic of currency informs the plot of *That Man Bolt*. Finally, in *Cleopatra Jones and the Casino of Gold*, the eponymous special agent faces a casino owner who controls most of the local heroin trade.

The depiction of Macao as a pit of forbidden pleasures and rampant moral corruption was in line with Hollywood's traditionally Eurocentric portrayal of colonized areas. The rise of cinema had coincided with the height of imperialism and, from early on, the film industry had reflected the interests and prejudices of the hegemonic nations, idealizing the West's role in pushing back the frontiers of ignorance, disease and tyranny.[27] As part of this process, American films had incorporated an orientalist narrative and visual tropes inherited from the works of European explorers, novelists and painters, which had proven popular with the public. Classic cinema presented a clear dichotomy between East and West, displaying little interest in intercultural understanding. It typically rendered non-Western cultures and regions as strange, perverse, mysterious, romantic, dangerous (if ultimately submissive) and on the whole opposed to the values of modernity and rationality personified by Western protagonists. This representation implicitly, and sometimes explicitly, supported the rhetoric of American and European imperial powers who justified colonialism as

---

[26] *Kill a Dragon*, 30:35–45.
[27] As argued by Robert Stam in *Film Theory: An Introduction* (Malden, MA: Blackwell Publishing, 2000), pp. 19–20.

a philanthropic effort to control and civilize so-called primitive lands and peoples.[28]

Nevertheless, the Portuguese regime did not find in American movies a clear endorsement of its presence in Macao.[29] For one thing, while genre conventions led to the perpetuation of earlier stereotypes, after the end of the Second World War mainstream cinema had begun to evolve into more politically complex directions, gradually and often ambivalently mixing colonialist images with anti-colonialist sensibilities.[30] More significantly for the corpus of films analysed in this article, Hollywood's gaze was not concerned with Portugal's perspective. Reflecting their semi-peripheral status in the cartography of the world's powers, the Portuguese settlers were either wholly disregarded or relegated to act as mere intermediaries in the orientalist adventures of American characters (and one Eurasian protagonist, in the case of *Love Is a Many-Splendored Thing*).[31] As a result, the ways in which Portuguese rule was represented were not always favourable, as indicated by a closer analysis of the major American film productions of the 1950s to feature Macao.

Hollywood's highest profile work to engage extensively with the Portuguese colony, the classic film noir *Macao*,[32] came about as the result of multiple creative voices. Howard Hughes, head of the production company RKO Pictures, bought the story rights from screenwriter Bob Williams in August 1949.[33] Josef von Sternberg unenthusiastically signed up to direct the film and

---

[28] The key text on the origins and fundaments of orientalist discourse remains Edward Said, *Orientalism* (New York: Pantheon, 1978). For an extended discussion of Hollywood's ethnocentrism, including towards Asia, see Gina Marchetti, *Romance and the Yellow Peril: Race, Sex, and Discursive Strategies in Hollywood Fiction* (Berkeley: University of California Press, 1993); Ella Shohat and Robert Stam, *Unthinking Eurocentrism: Multiculturalism and the Media* (London and New York: Routledge, 1994); *Visions of the East: Orientalism in Film*, ed. by Matthew Bernstein and Gaylyn Studlar (London: Rutgers, 1997).

[29] During the Estado Novo dictatorship, the censorship office would only allow *Kill a Dragon* to air in Portugal if references to the Portuguese gangster and the Mafia of Macao were cut out, according to documents in the Torre do Tombo national archive (IAN/TT/SNI, IGAC (2ªinc), cx342, Nº464, Dispatch from 13 July 1968). It did not allow *Smuggler's Island* to air at all (IAN/TT/SNI, IGAC (1ªinc), cx342, Nº22145, Dispatch from 28 February 1952). The remaining films are not listed in the censorship archive, which means either that they were not purchased by Portuguese distributors or that their files, like many official documents from the time, have been lost.

[30] Jon Cowans, *Empire Films and the Crisis of Colonialism, 1946–1959* (Baltimore, MD: Johns Hopkins University Press, 2015).

[31] The other exception, as early as the 1960s, are the two Chinese children at the forefront of *Out of the Tiger's Mouth*. In fact, this was a particularly original production, not only because it was an independent film shot entirely on location in Macao and Hong Kong, but because for once the indictment of living conditions in the colony comes across as purposefully critical rather than incidental to the plot. For details of the film's production, see the promotional pamphlet by Blank-Rand Associates, Public Relations, at the New York Museum of Modern Art, Film Study Center, Out of the Tiger's Mouth, *News from BR*.

[32] Academic debate over the exact parameters of the film noir genre remains inconclusive. Although not a perfectly archetypal example of the genre, *Macao* has nevertheless been included in canonical lists such as *Film Noir: An Encyclopaedic Reference to the American Style*, ed. by Alain Silver and Elizabeth M. Ward (New York: Overlook Press, 1979), pp. 179–80, and Spencer Selby, *Dark City: The Film Noir* (Jefferson, NC: McFarland & Company, 1984), p. 160.

[33] 'STORY BUYS', *Variety*, 15 August 1949.

his work was well underway by the time he was fired, owing to disputes with the cast. Hughes, who had a reputation for interfering with the content of RKO's films, then hired uncredited director Nicholas Ray to shoot retakes and additional scenes. Script credit went to Stanley Rubin and Bernard Schoenfeld, although there were six other writers involved in the script's various drafts, including last-minute rewrites by leading actor Robert Mitchum.[34] As explained below, Hollywood's trade organization, the Motion Picture Association of America (MPAA), also had a significant input into the final product. Among the transformations brought about by this turbulent production history, the film's tone seems to have shifted dramatically. At the outbreak of the Korean War, *Variety* reported that RKO was eager to exploit this military conflict by working it into *Macao*'s screenplay.[35] The project's perceived topicality got the film rushed into production in the summer of 1950.[36] However, no signs of either Korea or the war made it to the shooting script, much less to the final cut of the film, released in April 1952.[37]

If anything, on the surface the end product seemed decisively apolitical. It told an escapist story of intrigue and romance close to China's border without any reference to the fact that US troops were at the time fighting against the Chinese. The byzantine plot follows three Americans who arrive in Macao simultaneously: wandering veteran Nick Cochran (Robert Mitchum); gambling salesman Lawrence C. Trumble (William Bendix), who is actually an undercover New York police officer; and worldly singer Julie Benton (Jane Russel), who gets hired at a casino owned by American racketeer Vincent Halloran (Brad Dexter). Trumble sets in motion a convoluted plan involving a smuggled diamond necklace in order to lure Halloran into international waters, where the International Police can arrest him. A love triangle between Halloran, Julie and Nick, combined with a misplaced suspicion regarding the identity of the undercover agent, leads Halloran to kidnap Nick. The web of double-crosses and misunderstandings is further complicated by Halloran's jealous girlfriend Margie (Gloria Grahame) and the improbably named Felizardo José Espírito Sebastian (Thomas Gomez), a crooked Portuguese police lieutenant working for Halloran on the side. In the end, Nick escapes, delivers Halloran to the International Police and gets together with Julie.

In the screenplay, the plot and dialogue presented an unflattering image of Portuguese rule, but this was deliberately toned down due to the interference of the MPAA's Production Code Administration (PCA). The PCA, headed by Joseph Breen, was in charge of enforcing the film industry's moralistic self-

---

[34] John Baxter, *Von Sternberg* (Lexington: University Press of Kentucky, 2010), pp. 244–49; *Macao*'s entry on the AFI Catalog of Feature Films <http://www.afi.com/members/catalog/DetailView.aspx?s=&Movie=50564> [accessed 27 September 2014].
[35] 'H'wood Scurries', *Variety*, 5 July 1950, p. 22
[36] 'RKO Speeds "Macao" As Topical, Timely Fare', *Variety*, 17 July 1950.
[37] American Film Scripts Online [AFSO], 'Macao Shooting Script' <http://solomon.afso.alexanderstreet.com/cgi-bin/asp/philo/afso/overview.pl?FS001033> [accessed 27 September 2014].

censorship, operating under the Motion Picture Production Code.[38] Having read *Macao*'s proposed screenplay, in July 1950 Breen ruled the basic story unacceptable. Besides the 'low tone of criminality' and several lurid details, PCA reviewers argued that the project violated a section of the Production Code which stated that the 'history, institutions, prominent people and citizenry of all nations shall be represented fairly'. Specifically, they unanimously objected to the treatment of the Chinese characters, saying: 'The whole flavour of the story tends to indicate that these "coolies" are little more than animals, and the element of "white supremacy" is, we feel, quite offensive.' They also objected to the depiction of the Portuguese administration:

> The picturization of the District of Macao is, we think, an unfair and unjust characterization of the Portuguese. All, or nearly all, of the officials of the District portrayed in this picture are shown to be criminally dishonest. This has reference, specifically, to the Police Lieutenant, Sebastian, and, by implication at least, all the other law-enforcing bodies on the Island.[39]

The PCA's input was detailed and insistent. Breen suggested that RKO consult with Addison Durland — the PCA's Latin American advisor, considered the most suited in the office staff to advise on Portugal[40] — over the 'improper characterization' of the Portuguese and Chinese.[41] In point of fact, some of the PCA's demands seemed more concerned with avoiding controversy and accusations of bigotry than with actual fairness and accuracy — after all, the image of widespread corruption among Macao's police and civil servants was not far-fetched, according to the internal account of Portugal's own intelligence services.[42] Even so, among other requests, the PCA asked the producers to omit the police's dismissive and, in one scene, brutal behaviour towards the Chinese population, as well as to avoid indications of corruption by not showing Lt Sebastian in a Rolls-Royce or a banknote in a customs official's hands.[43] Likewise, the introductory narration establishing Macao was to be rewritten, 'having in mind a fair-minded approach in dealing with the description of this colony'.[44]

The PCA's impact, however, was limited by the producers' awareness that the territory's seedy connotation was one of the project's key selling points to the

---

[38] For a detailed analysis of Joseph Breen's role as director of the PCA, see Thomas Doherty, *Hollywood's Censor: Joseph I. Breen & the Production Code Administration* (New York: Columbia University Press, 2007).
[39] AMPAS, MPAA, PCA records, *Macao*, Letter from Joseph Breen to Harold Melniker, 11 July 1950.
[40] For Durland's background, see Brian O'Neil, 'The Demands of Authenticity: Addison Durland and Hollywood's Latin Images during World War II', in *Classic Hollywood, Classic Whiteness*, ed. by Daniel Bernardi (Minneapolis: University of Minnesota Press, 2001), pp. 359–61. At the time, Durland also consulted on the Portugal-set production *The Miracle of Our Lady of Fatima*. — AMPAS, MPAA, PCA records, *Miracle of Fatima*, Letter from Joseph Breen to Kenneth Clark, 13 November 1952.
[41] AMPAS, MPAA, PCA records, *Macao*, Breen to Melniker, 11 July 1950.
[42] Zhiliang, p. 326.
[43] AMPAS, MPAA, PCA records, *Macao*, Breen to Melniker, 11 July 1950 and 28 July 1950.
[44] AMPAS, MPAA, PCA records, *Macao*, Breen to Melniker, 13 July 1951.

thrill-seeking public.[45] Although the scripted scenes most explicitly disrespectful of the Portuguese rulers were left out of the film,[46] other concessions to the Production Code remained quite superficial. For example, the brief inclusion of a low-ranking Portuguese officer of the International Police, who was on screen for just twenty-two seconds,[47] his back turned to the camera and uttering one inconsequential line of dialogue, was enough to counterbalance Lt Sebastian's substantial role in the story, thus satisfying the PCA that the Portuguese in the film were fairly portrayed, both sympathetically and unsympathetically.[48]

Orientalist themes and imagery were not novel in the film noir genre,[49] or even in Josef von Sternberg's own body of work,[50] but *Macao* set out to establish a distinctive identity for its location from the start. The film opens with shots of boats and sampans along the Macao coast during daytime, while a documentary-style voice-over delivers the PCA-approved initial narration.[51] At first, this almost sounds like a Portuguese propaganda broadcast, even down to the luso-tropicalist emphasis on the colony's peculiarity and racial mixture, in line with what was becoming Lisbon's official discourse about its empire:

> This is Macao: a fabulous speck on the Earth's surface, just off the south coast of China, a 35-mile boat trip from Hong Kong. It is an ancient Portuguese colony, quaint and bizarre. The crossroads of the Far East, its population a mixture of all races and nationalities, mostly Chinese. Macao, often called the 'Monte Carlo of the Orient'...[52]

It quickly becomes clear that the difference between Macao and Monte Carlo — typically depicted by Hollywood as the luxurious site of elitist casinos and hotels[53] — is more than merely geographical. As the footage changes to night-time, the camera travels along dark, crowded streets, ill-lit by neon signs and shabby stalls, leading to a foot chase that will culminate in the murder of an American agent, knifed in the back by a Chinese thug. The voice-over informs the viewer:

---

[45] This aspect is repeatedly highlighted in the Exhibitor's Campaign Book provided by RKO to UK distributors to help promote the movie. One section states: 'The angles which lend themselves to pay-off exploitation are self-evident: triple star power, volcanic romance, music, thrills and the fascinating atmosphere of the East.' — British Film Institute, Reuben Library, *Macao* Pressbook.
[46] AFSO, 'Macao Shooting Script' — In an early sequence, Nick would have rescued a drowning Chinese worker, only to be yelled at by a Portuguese boat captain for having delayed his ferry (pp. 3–6). Another cut scene included a Portuguese aristocrat, Senhor Garcia, who helped out Trumble and said of Sebastian and Halloran, 'Someday our city will be free of men like that' (pp. 105–08). The script ended with Sebastian, fired and disgraced, leaving Macao with a sardonic call-back to an earlier line: 'And so I bid farewell to beautiful Macao — always friendly and hospitable' (p. 123).
[47] *Macao*, 51:14–36.
[48] AMPAS, MPAA, PCA records, *Macao*, Analysis Chart, 25 January 1952.
[49] James Naremore, *More than Night: Film Noir in its Contexts* (Berkeley: University of California Press, 1998), pp. 225–27.
[50] Von Sternberg had directed the China-set dramas *Shanghai Express* (1932) and *The Shanghai Gesture* (1941). For a detailed analysis of those works, see Baxter, pp. 142–51 and 230–36.
[51] AMPAS, MPAA, PCA records, *Macao*, Breen to Melniker, 27 December 1951.
[52] *Macao*, 01:24–52.
[53] See, for example, *The Young in Heart*, Dir. Richard Wallace, United Artists, 1938, or *Rebecca*, Dir. Alfred Hitchcock, United Artists, 1940.

[Macao] has two faces: one calm and open, the other veiled and secret. Here millions in gold and diamonds change hands, some across the gambling tables, some mysteriously in the night. Macao is a fugitives' haven, for at the three-mile limit the authority of the International Police comes to an end.[54]

The 'two faces' of Macao are reinforced aesthetically throughout the film. Some scenes are worthy of a travelogue, presenting the colony as a picturesque, dream-like — if inhospitably hot — setting. Examples include the lingering and brightly lit shots of the boats and harbour upon the characters' arrival in Macao,[55] as well as the background footage of the city and docks during Julie and Nick's romantic interlude halfway through the story.[56] Conversely, in the film's final act, which takes place wholly at night, the chiaroscuro black-and-white cinematography — characteristic of film noir and of von Sternberg's earlier forays into German expressionism[57] — creates a sinister atmosphere of violence and occult forces hiding in the stark shadows. This is particularly the case during a climatic chase — echoing the opening sequence — where Nick runs desperately among sampans and fishnets, and Trumble ends up fatally stabbed.[58]

Besides the initial voice-over and the duality motif, the film uses multiple strategies to convey Macao's distinctiveness. The poster's tagline speaks of 'exotic, exciting MACAO, port of sin and shady dealings!'[59] Gambling is presented as not merely a leisure activity but an all-consuming lifestyle: the customs officer declares that 'In Macao everything is a gamble'; the clerk at 'Hotel Portugueza' informs Trumble that gambling halls have no opening hours because they never close; Julie feels frustrated when her seductive singing act fails to shift the casino customers' attention away from the games.[60] The crowd at the gambling tables is also not the same as in Monte Carlo: the wealthy sit on an upper gallery, above the masses, looking down on the tables and lowering their bids in baskets (a visual von Sternberg had used before in the Chinese casino of *The Shanghai Gesture*). Moreover, most scenes were filmed in the studio, with the little genuine footage of the colony being either projected onto the background or used for wider establishing shots.[61] The set design highlights Macao's particular colonizing history: the decor of Halloran's casino combines Chinese dragons and Portuguese guitars; the docks where Nick is kidnapped appear to be a prototypical Hollywood Eastern-looking backlot,[62]

---

[54] *Macao*, 01:52–02:17.
[55] *Macao*, 10:15–11:13.
[56] *Macao*, 37:37–41:55.
[57] Lotte H. Eisner, *The Haunted Screen: Expressionism in the German Cinema and the Influence of Max Reinhardt*, 2nd edn (California: University of California Press, 2008), p. 314.
[58] *Macao*, 1:07:34–.11:56.
[59] Ad in *Variety*, 2 May 1952, p. 5.
[60] *Macao*, 13:51–52, 23:20–22, and 32:53–33:02.
[61] A second unit on location lensed more than 20,000 feet of original footage in the summer of 1950. — 'RKO Speeds "Macao"...', *Variety*, 17 July 1950.
[62] A memo by the film's executive producer states that it 'appears to be the backlot at Cost Plus Imports' — AMPAS, General Collection, Macao, Memo from Samuel Bischoff [no date].

but the *mise-en-scène* and Mitchum's acting make a point of drawing attention to the Portuguese street name sign that reads 'Largo Do Pagode Da Barra'.[63] Nevertheless, overall the orientalist iconography far outweighs the Portuguese, from the soundtrack to the title's font during the opening credits, as well as the wardrobe, with a clear contrast between the light-coloured suits of the Westerners and the black-clad Asian characters and extras.

Ultimately, despite the PCA's efforts, the truly distinguishing feature of Macao, as presented in the film, is its feeble law enforcement. The dialogue keeps reminding the viewer of the colony's nefarious reputation.[64] The plot rests on the central premise that Macao is — as the voice-over puts it — 'a fugitives' haven', where police detectives are killed with impunity and the only way to arrest a racketeer is to get him leave the local jurisdiction. Portuguese authorities come across as eagerly corruptible. Following the PCA's request, a customs officer is no longer explicitly bribed with money, but he nevertheless accepts a pack of cigars from Trumble while examining his luggage.[65] Moreover, Halloran blithely orders Lt Sebastian around.[66] Although the script describes the short and chubby Sebastian as 'a handsome middle-aged Portuguese, debonair and corruptible, but withal a shrewd official',[67] Gomez plays him as pompous, cowardly and generally buffoonish. By contrast, the brief scenes set outside Macao's three-mile limit take place in contexts of stern authority: first the Hong Kong headquarters of the International Criminal Police Commission, headed by the British Commander Stewart, and then an International Police ship in which Stewart is accompanied by two subordinate officers — the Chinese Mr Chang and the Portuguese Mr Alvaris.[68] This disparity suggests a Portuguese inability to rule the colony alone and the need for outside assistance to impose order. Thus, while the film's most orientalist tropes are reserved for Asian characters, the Portuguese themselves appear as a version of the 'barbaric other', at once semi-colonizers and semi-colonized, a view which was reinforced in Hollywood's subsequent output.

Three years after the release of *Macao*, two other big productions featured the Portuguese colony, albeit with much shorter screen time. Nominated for eight Oscars, including Best Picture, *Love is a Many-Splendored Thing* is a melodrama directed by Henry King and adapted by John Patrick from a 1952 autobiographical novel by Han Suyin. The film is set in Hong Kong during

---

[63] *Macao*, 51:37–47.
[64] When Trumble asks Julie if this is her first trip to Macao, she answers 'From what I hear once is once too often' and he acknowledges 'So I've heard...' (07:50–54). Later, asked by Nick if she is smuggling anything into the country, Julie replies 'The way I hear it, you smuggle things out of here, not in' (12:21–28). When they first meet, Lt Sebastian tells Nick that 'It is our fond hope that all visitors to Macao should feel as untroubled here as Adam in the Garden of Eden', to which Nick remarks 'Untroubled? It ain't the way I heard it' (15:42–53).
[65] *Macao*, 13:40–46.
[66] *Macao*, 56:38–57:55.
[67] AFSO, 'Macao Shooting Script', p. 15.
[68] *Macao*, 03:22–04:08 and 50:27–51:36.

1949 and 1950, against the background of the refugee crisis that followed the Chinese Revolution. It tells the story of Eurasian Doctor Han Suyin's (Jennifer Jones) love affair with married American correspondent Mark Elliott (William Holden), who dies in the Korean War. Also capitalizing on McCarthy-era anti-Chinese sentiment, *Soldier of Fortune* is an adventure drama directed by Edward Dmytryk and scripted by Ernest K. Gann from his own 1954 novel. The plot concerns Jane Hoyt's (Susan Hayward) efforts to find her husband Louis (Gene Barry), a photojournalist imprisoned in China as a suspected spy. In Hong Kong, Jane falls in love with shipping magnate and alleged smuggler Hank Lee (Clark Gable). Hank undertakes a dangerous rescue operation into Chinese territory, in order to allow Jane to resolve her marital relationship before committing to staying with him.[69]

These films are mostly set in Hong Kong and portray it as strikingly different from the Macao at the centre of Josef von Sternberg's film noir. Shot in bright yet realistic colours, the British colony seems crowded but orderly, a metropolis that smoothly combines skyscrapers and sampan communities.[70] In *Soldier of Fortune*, a representative of the American consulate informs Jane from the onset that the local authorities are competent and cooperative.[71] The well-disciplined Maritime Police, which peacefully patrols the sampans, is personified by the British Inspector Merryweather (Michael Rennie), shown to be honest, perceptive and brave. The film even makes a point of justifying how a smuggler like Hank can operate out of a British colony by having Merryweather explain that Hong Kong is 'a few miles of land, yes, but just outside the waters are Chinese. There they do as they please and so does Hank Lee. Inside the colony, he is very careful.'[72] In *Love is a Many-Splendored Thing*, Han Suyin works in an efficient British-run hospital with spacious facilities, modern resources and a helpful staff. Despite depicting Hong Kong as a stable, functioning society, the film contrasts the settlers' conservative attitudes with the idealistic liberalism of the American Mark Elliot, thus implicitly legitimizing the US presence in Asia as an 'enlightened' alternative to British rule.[73] Nevertheless, in both movies the central contrast is ultimately between Western freedom in Hong Kong and communist tyranny in China, privileging an anti-communist message over an anti-colonialist one.[74]

[69] For production notes on the films, see the entries at the AFI Catalog of Feature Films — <http://www.afi.com/members/catalog/DetailView.aspx?s=&Movie=51570> and <http://www.afi.com/members/catalog/DetailView.aspx?s=&Movie=51663> [accessed 28 September 2014].
[70] Hollywood depictions of Hong Kong were more varied than the ones in the films under discussion. However, since these were productions that also depicted Macao, they did invite a direct comparison and serve as the most patent form of contextualization of the Portuguese colony in American film fiction.
[71] *Soldier of Fortune*, 04:25–05:03.
[72] *Soldier of Fortune*, 11:08–40. In fact, although Merryweather accuses Hank of being a gangster, Hank acts more like an archetypal hero than the anti-hero suggested by the film's title: he has adopted three orphans, helps the local community, and comes across as suave, noble and lucid.
[73] For an extended discussion of this dimension of the film, see Marchetti, pp. 109–24.
[74] For a closer look at this aspect, see Cowans, pp. 212–13, 215–16.

Regarding the neighbouring colony, each film suggests a different facet of semi-peripheral colonization. When Macao shows up in *Love is a Many-Splendored Thing*, its story function is exceptionally benign compared to other Hollywood narratives. Han Suyin elopes to Macao to spend a romantic week alone with Mark, only to find a welcoming and touristic city. The two lovers stay in a comfortable hotel, eat in a restaurant with moody saxophone music and have their future read by a professional fortune teller. They are served by friendly Portuguese staff, illustrating Portugal's role as tolerant facilitator of its allies' desires.[75] Conversely, in *Soldier of Fortune* Jane goes to Macao following a lead on her missing husband that takes her to the Portuguese Fernand Rocha (Mel Welles), who runs a language school in Rua da Felicidade.[76] Fernand tricks Jane into writing him a $500 traveller's cheque, holds her captive, and spends the money on gambling and women, brashly slapping his female Chinese partner when she complains. Jane is rescued by Hank, who barges in and violently beats up the feeble Fernand, now representing the Portuguese as decadent rulers in need of outside discipline.[77] The overall impression is summed up in a dialogue exchange as the two protagonists reunite: Hank asks 'Why did you come to a place like this without me? Are you alright?' and Jane meekly pleads 'Take me away from here.'[78]

Visually, the approaches of the two productions are also distinct. *Love is a Many-Splendored Thing* seeks to create a romantic atmosphere through orientalist fetishization, lingering on scenic shots of the Macao harbour, a traditional funeral procession and the mystic rituals of the Asian fortune teller.[79] *Soldier of Fortune*'s engagement with the location is more superficial: its Macao sequence does not include any actual footage of the colony, relying entirely on a modest studio version with obvious props (a fado guitar, Portuguese street signs).[80] Nevertheless, the humble decor of dimly-lit alleys displayed during an extended shot of Jane and Hank walking down the empty ersatz-Rua da Felicidade, at dawn, underlines Macao's gloomy connotation in the story.[81] Thus each film draws on one of the 'two faces' described in *Macao*'s opening voice-over — one highlights the 'calm and open' face, the other focuses on its 'veiled and secret' face.

Although elements of this duality can be found across smaller productions as well, 1950s' B movies always put greater emphasis on Macao's seamier side. Indeed, the remaining films can be considered 'exploitation movies',

[75] *Love is a Many-Splendored Thing*, 1:09:35–20:07.
[76] Although probably meant to be the Portuguese name 'Fernando', the sign on the door identifies him as 'Fernand'.
[77] *Soldier of Fortune*, 55:51–59:11 and 1:09.14–12:46.
[78] *Soldier of Fortune*, 1:11:53–12:01.
[79] *Love is a Many-Splendored Thing*, 1:09:35–55; 1:12:59–13:55; 1:16:26–18:30.
[80] Susan Hayward was unable to leave the US because her ex-husband refused to let her take their sons with her, so Dmytryk had to shoot all her scenes in Los Angeles. — Chrystopher J. Spicer, *Clark Gable: Biography, Filmography, Bibliography* (Jefferson, NC: McFarland & Company, 2002), p. 266.
[81] *Soldier of Fortune*, 1:12:46–13:55.

i.e. relatively low-budget projects that, lacking star power or high production values, sought audience appeal through the choice of sensationalist subject matter. Even when presenting a murkier depiction of Hong Kong, those films associate the British island with a superior exercise of power compared to its Portuguese neighbour. In *Hong Kong Confidential*, an intelligence division in Hong Kong sends an American and a British agent on an undercover mission to Macao, where an abducted Middle Eastern prince is being secretly held by a gangster working for the Soviet Union. Both *Flight to Hong Kong* and *The Scavengers* feature earnest police inspectors concerned with smuggling in the Crown colony. In the former film, the inspector addresses viewers directly, before the opening credits, breaking the fourth wall to explain that the Hong Kong Police Constabulary is part of an international effort to stop a worldwide smuggling syndicate.[82] The plot focuses on a cell of this syndicate comfortably operating out of Macao — the Portuguese authorities are nowhere to be seen, but the criminals are apprehended by the police when they meet in Hong Kong, at the end of the movie. By contrasting Portugal's ineffective rule with the British hegemonic model, these films further cast Portuguese colonialism in a subaltern light.

In conclusion, the image of the Portuguese empire in North American film fiction was overwhelmingly restricted to the Asian colony of Macao, which garnered particular attention in the 1950s. In line with Hollywood's orientalist tradition, the stories focused on Anglo-American leads engaging, on the one hand, with the setting's seductiveness and, on the other, with its perils and loose morals. The Portuguese presence, if acknowledged at all, may seem almost incidental to the stories, yet these films inevitably produced a discourse about Portugal's empire, at the very least by virtue of being set in it. Implied in the two faces of Macao conveyed by Hollywood, especially by the major productions, was a semi-peripheral condition of the Portuguese colonial project, midway between the hegemonic centre and the subaltern periphery. The films presented Portuguese colonialism as at its best when welcoming visitors and providing an attractive landscape for their romance (Nick and Julie in *Macao*; Suyin and Mark in *Love is a Many-Splendored Thing*), and at its worst when failing to restrain local crime and thus to protect western outsiders (Jane in *Soldier of Fortune*; Nick, Trumble and the murdered American policeman in *Macao*). The latter trait is particularly striking when compared to the image of order and safety linked to the British colony of Hong Kong in the same films.

While this subtext of the Portuguese as model hosts but comparatively unfit rulers ascribes, on a purely representational level, a subaltern status to Portugal's empire, it also demands a multifaceted reading of Western orientalism. By portraying Macao as the 'wickedest city' in the world, these movies were not only building on stereotypes associated with an orientalist view of the East, but also conjuring an indirect indictment of its colonizers,

---

[82] *Flight to Hong Kong*, 01:26–02:15.

who were, by implication, unable to fulfil their self-styled mission of promoting Western civilization. Yet Portugal's inefficacy was not merely implied by the compromised state of the colony. The most prominent Portuguese characters (Felizardo Sebastian, Fernand Rocha) were actually shown to be highly corrupt and duplicitous, if ultimately submissive. In other words, Hollywood's exoticist impulses were not restricted to the Asian dimension of Macao — they also reflected a form of orientalization of its southern European rulers. Thus, in its very limited exposure through the lenses of classic American cinema, Portuguese colonialism came across as inadequate and problematic, although it was more visibly maligned for being Portuguese than for being colonialism.

The research leading to this article was funded by the Fundação para a Ciência e Tecnologia (grant SFRH/BPD/85145/2012).

Censored and Banned: Portuguese Films during the Government of Marcello Caetano (1968–74)

ANA BELA MORAIS

Centro de Estudos Comparatistas, Faculdade de Letras, Universidade de Lisboa

Introduction

Marcello Caetano replaced António Salazar as President of the Council of Ministers (i.e. Prime Minister) of Portugal in September 1968. When this happened there was an expectation that the regime would modernize and open up politically, to the point that there would no longer be a system of censorship in Portugal, but this hope proved illusory.

Elections were announced for October 1969, and opposition forces were of the view that they could only be considered legitimate if censorship were to end. However, in that same year Marcello Caetano unequivocally defended the retention of censorship. His main argument was that the conduct of the colonial wars required the home front to be protected from 'psychological campaigns' that could endanger the front line. He gave the additional justification that any other country in the same position would adopt similar measures. A further argument that he repeatedly and insistently employed was that there was a lack of readiness amongst both the middle class and the working class, due to the many years that censorship had been in force, and that there was therefore a real need for a period of transition for the country to prepare itself for life without censorship.[1] As for the elections, they showed without a shadow of doubt that censorship still existed: the manipulation and suppression of the results led to an unequivocal victory for the candidates of the União Nacional.

The idea that the system of censorship might be abolished with Marcello Caetano's coming to power was not entirely groundless, since one of first measures he took, in 1968, was to abolish the Secretariado Nacional de Informação, Cultura Popular e Turismo (usually known as the SNI). It was replaced by the Secretaria de Estado da Informação e Turismo (SEIT), led by Moreira Baptista, who had been chairman of the Comissão de Exame e Classificação de Espectáculos in the 1960s. However, although the National Assembly had agreed, in 1970, to look at the regime of prior censorship,

---

[1] Marcello Caetano, *Estado social* (Lisbon: Secretaria de Estado da Informação e Turismo, 1970), p. 21.

after two years a new law was passed which relaxed only superficially the previous limitations on the freedom of the press. The Direcção dos Serviços de Censura was replaced by the Direcção-Geral da Informação, which required all newspapers and periodicals to bear the phrase 'exame prévio' [prior examination], where previously had appeared 'censura' [censorship].[2] Films, too, whether locally made or entering Portugal from abroad, were subject to prior censorship.

In Portugal the Comissão de Censura answered directly to the SNI, and was constituted of a dozen censors nominated by the Prime Minister. Their job was to view and approve (or otherwise) all films and other public entertainments. The Portuguese state itself started to produce films in 1935, through the medium of the Secretariado da Propaganda Nacional, which was renamed the SNI with effect from 1944.

In this article I aim to examine the way in which the censorship of films was exercised in Portugal during the time of Marcello Caetano, by asking various questions. Which were the themes most often censored? How many films were censored and how many banned outright, and why? Did the beginning of the Caetano period mark a relaxation in what could be shown in Portuguese cinemas? By seeking answers to these questions I hope to contribute to a broader understanding of this period in Portuguese history.

The present investigation is based on a study of the archives of the Secretaria de Estado da Informação e Turismo (SEIT). All the information produced by the Comissão de Exame e Classificação de Espectáculos under the Estado Novo is to be found in the relevant section of the Arquivo Nacional da Torre do Tombo (ANTT), in Lisbon. As well as looking at the handling of the censorship of films, this investigation is also based on the study of the Actas da Comissão de Censura corresponding to the period from late 1971 to 25 April 1974.[3]

The case files dealing with the censorship of films reveal the way that the censors operated, including the views expressed on films and the representations and appeals made, as well as the censors' final reports. The Actas da Comissão de Censura constitute a summary of the proceedings of the Comissão de Censura, which was convened in order to discuss films and plays considered particularly problematical. As will be shown and exemplified through the course of this study, films that were prohibited or which raised doubts with respect to their classification were discussed during these meetings.

The study of film censorship under the Estado Novo in general, and during the time of Marcello Caetano in particular, is still at an early stage. This is mainly due to the fact that documents relating to censorship found in the Palácio Foz

---

[2] Jorge Ramos do Ó, 'Censura', in *Dicionário de história do Estado Novo*, ed. by Fernando Rosas and J. M. Brandão de Brito, 2 vols (Lisbon: Círculo de leitores, 1996), I, 139–41.
[3] According to Paulo Tremoceiro, in charge of material on censorship at the ANTT, the minute books of the Comissão de Censura covering the early period of the Caetano government (late 1968 to 1971) are not to be found in the archives. He does not know what happened to them, but notes that other documents also went missing in the period after the 25 April 1974 revolution.

— former headquarters of the Secretariado de Propaganda Nacional (SPN), the SNI and the SEIT — were only placed in the national archive (ANTT) in 2006, and so were only available to scholars from that date.[4] This study therefore sets out to present the results of a novel investigation.

In the first part of this study we shall present and examine the cases of Portuguese films that were censored, and in the second part those that were banned. Finally we shall draw some tentative conclusions — always provisional, of course, and open to later re-evaluation. Although there were films which were categorically banned and/or censored, there were others that were first refused but which, after representations were made, were then approved without cuts, for example. Given the complicated nature of these cases, the numbers for films that were censored or banned can only be given approximately, but even so they are of considerable importance for understanding society and mentality under the Caetano regime.

Portuguese Films that Were Censored, or Nearly...

Portuguese cinematic output prior to the April 1974 revolution was not abundant. The unfavourable economic circumstances, and, more importantly, the limits imposed on freedom of expression so characteristic of the Estado Novo, did not allow the production of many films.

Under the Estado Novo, Portuguese cinematic production divided between two distinct tendencies. There was a cinema allied to the regime, and therefore conformist, and a cinema of resistance, one that included the neo-realist tendency of Manuel Guimarães and the generation of the Portuguese New Cinema. As products of the same society, these two types of cinema cannot be considered completely opposed to one another, but they do demonstrate aesthetic and stylistic differences, which each look on the Portuguese culture and society of the time with a deliberately chosen and distinctive focus.

Censorship of the press, theatre and cinema was more rigorous than that of books, since the former were seen as artistic and cultural expression for the masses, ones that communicated more directly with the public. First Salazar and then Caetano were fully cognizant of this difference, and for this reason filmmakers of the time — whether directing films aligned with the regime or working independently — were forced into self-censorship to secure the approval of their films.

Throughout the period of the Estado Novo, a film producer had to put forward ideas that satisfied not only possible commercial backers but also the Fundo do Cinema Nacional (FCN), which from 1948 gave partial financial support to those projects it agreed to back.[5] However, the creation of the FCN,

---

[4] Ana Bela Morais, 'Recensão crítica do livro *Cinema e censura em Portugal*, de Lauro António (2001)', *Aniki. Revista Portuguesa da Imagem em Movimento*, 1.1 (2014), 104–07; available online at <http://aim.org.pt/ojs/index.php/revista/article/view/31>.

[5] For detailed information on the Fundo do Cinema Nacional, see Fausto Cruchinho, 'O Conselho do

with state support, rather than stimulating the production of Portuguese films created a dependency on the regime that resulted in an even greater degradation in commercial cinema. It was only with the creation of the Centro Português de Cinema (CPC), in 1971, supported until 1974 by the Calouste Gulbenkian Foundation, and also with the passing of law no. 7/71, published on 7 December 1971, that Portuguese cinema was able to progressively free itself from a dependency on the market and become a vehicle for artistic expression. However, by gaining at this period a certain independence from public taste, and facing also difficulties in securing the distribution of films — since there was no exhibition circuit supported by the state — Portuguese cinema became little known to the wider public, and little understood by it.

The existence of strict political and moral censorship prevented the showing in Portugal of some of the great works of François Truffaut and Jean-Luc Godard, a fact that contributed to the poor reception given to the Portuguese New Cinema, itself much influenced by the French *Nouvelle Vague*. Not being familiar with the style of cinema, the majority of Portuguese failed to understand either the aesthetics or the innovative message of those films. The public reluctance to accept the films made in the context of the Portuguese New Cinema can also be explained by the inherent characteristics of this type of film. The producers of this generation, in the 1960s, avoided direct confrontation with the censors by an evasive aesthetic, using a metaphorical and elliptical language that did not say openly what it meant to say. This characteristic is not only political but also aesthetic. As Luís de Pina comments:

> Obviously censorship does not prevent the development of talent any more than its absence stimulates it, but the truth is that cinematic output suffers from prohibition and learns a language of allusion, of implying, of understatement, always failing to lay out matters clearly. It could also create — and amongst us it did create — a fear of addressing questions, sticking to the superficial, the documental, the conventional.[6]

Portuguese New Cinema, which started with films such as *Dom Roberto* (1962), by Ernesto de Sousa, and *Os verdes anos* (1963), by Paulo Rocha, represented a break with the cinema practised in Portugal up to then. It freed its characters from the stereotypical division into good and bad types and from the external moral code that imprisoned them, making them more complex by presenting their own internal dilemmas and personal responsibilities. The films of this period expressed themselves above all in existential terms, but by indicating a latent oppression they were able, by way of allusion, to put out an oppositional message, by refusing to deal directly with the political and social organization of the country at the time. Censorship even came to function as an incentive to the imagination; in this particular sense we can agree with

---

Cinema: notas sobre o seu funcionamento (1962–1971)', in *O cinema sob o olhar de Salazar*, ed. by Luís Reis Torgal (Lisbon: Temas e Debates, 2001), pp. 339–55 (p. 339).
[6] Luís de Pina, *A aventura do cinema português* (Lisbon: Editorial Vega, 1977), p. 137.

Bazin: 'the function of censorship is essential to dreaming as to cinema. It is dialectically constitutive.'[7] In this respect, it could be said that

> unlike the cine-club movement, which the Estado Novo, even in the Caetano period, did not hesitate to suppress, the so-called 'new cinema' was able, even before the 25 April, to control all, or nearly all the positions in the 'cinema' world, thus having in its hands the power to produce, to teach and to criticize, despite its political alignment to the left.[8]

Self-censorship took place when directors realized that their films would be cut, or even banned, if they were presented to the Comissão de Censura exactly as they had been made. The evidence given by José Fonseca e Costa, director of *O recado* (1970–72), and António de Macedo, regarding his film *A promessa* (1972), are examples of that perception of the need for self-censorship.[9]

Apart from explicit examples of self-censorship, which consisted of simply eliminating or modifying images and dialogue that the directors thought might be objectionable to the censors, there was also a more subtle form of self-censorship, which employed synecdochic or symbolic representations, that is, they made a figure stand in for a wider context. For example, in the *O Malamado* (1973), by Fernando Matos Silva, and *Brandos costumes* (1975), by Alberto Seixas Santos, we can see that the fathers represent metonymically the figure of Salazar, while their houses represent Portugal.[10]

As with foreign films, all Portuguese films had to go to the Comissão de Censura aos Espectáculos, which from 1957 became know as the Comissão de Exame e Classificação dos Espectáculos. As is indicated by the change of name, prior censorship of Portuguese film scripts ended, leaving only the requirement that the finished film be submitted. This change can perhaps be explained by the Commission's coming to understand that what they needed to censor was not the script, but rather the images and dialogue that were included in the completed film. However, this made self-censorship even more important, to make sure that the finished film could be shown without cuts.

Although there were various small changes over time, the system of censorship worked in one of two ways: initially there was the so-called 'prior' censorship of the intended scripts; later, there was the examination of all films on completion by the Comissão de Exame e Classificação de Espectáculos, which could impose cuts or even a total prohibition. Self-censorship, though, was another form which producers and directors were encouraged to adopt from the outset, to avoid having their films rejected. Finally there was also

---

[7] André Bazin, *Qu'est-ce que le cinéma?* (Paris: Cerf, 2002), p. 251.
[8] Paulo Filipe Monteiro, 'Uma margem no centro: a arte e o poder do "novo cinema"', in *O cinema sob o olhar de Salazar*, ed. by Luís Reis Torgal (Lisbon: Temas e Debates, 2001), pp. 306–38 (p. 306).
[9] See below for discussion of these films.
[10] For a more in-depth study of self-censorship in Portuguese cinema, see Ana Bela Morais 'Interdito e entre dito: reflexões em torno da autocensura na cinematografia portuguesa', in *Diálogos sobre censura e liberdade de expressão: Brasil e Portugal*, ed. by Maria Cristina Castilho Costa (São Paulo: Escola de Comunicações e Artes (ECA / USP), 2014), pp. 159–73.

the Fundo Nacional de Cinema, which chose the films to be supported by the Portuguese state.

Classifications by suitability for age were altered by Decree Law no. 263/71, of 18 June 1971, creating four ratings. Films classified A were deemed suitable for audiences over six years, B for those over ten, C for those over fourteen, and D for those over eighteen. The composition of the Comissão de Exame e Classificação de Espectáculos was also altered by the same Decree Law, being divided into two groups, one to deal with films and the other with plays. It also created an appeal board, independent of the Comissão, in which the respective Corporations were represented.[11]

Throughout the Estado Novo, the majority of Portuguese films were made for an audience that was regarded as uncultured and/or illiterate, for whom cinema should present role models that were morally appropriate and socially acceptable. Until the appearance of television, in 1957, cinema — along with radio — was one of the most all-embracing means of communication, and for this reason it was seen both by official ideology and by critics in general as a means of popular education. Not only was it desired that films should have this paternalistic streak, but the Comissão de Censura itself showed it, even correcting spelling mistakes in film scripts. By the 1970s the Comissão was allowing certain films to be shown, but in many cases only in studio cinemas, restricted to educated audiences; the showing of such films to the general public, in normal cinemas, remained prohibited, as happened with some of the films discussed below.

In the majority of Portuguese films of the 1950s, '60s and '70s the family is shown to be the nucleus of the social structure. Furthermore, the drama is never focused on a breakdown in the traditional family; for example, dramas based on adultery are very rare, which may perhaps be explained by the existence of censorship, whether of an official or a social kind. In the 1940s, the golden age of the regime's cinema, this was not a surprising. But even with the break represented by the New Cinema in the 1960s the family remains the nucleus, although from that moment on traditional society (and the family) was no longer represented in the same way. As stated before, these kinds of films expressed themselves above all in existential terms, refusing to deal directly with the political and social organization of the country at the time, and for that reason the way they handle the family structure is mostly quite subtle.

Any references to social problems were cut. Prior censorship of newspapers, for example, did not allow any reference to shanty towns; it was said that this was so that foreigners should not learn of them.[12] A brief scene in *O cerco* (1969), by António da Cunha Telles, was ordered cut because it showed barefooted children in the street.

---

[11] Ana Cabrera, 'A censura ao teatro no período marcelista', *Media & Jornalismo*, 12.7 (2008), 27–58 (p. 38).
[12] Cf. César Príncipe, *A censura de Salazar e Marcelo Caetano* (Lisbon: Caminho, 1999).

O cerco is the first film to deal with the theme of marital crisis. It tells the story of a young woman who has a lover, which leads to her separating from her husband after he physically assaults her. After this she has a number of relationships, different to those that her employer has tried to force upon her, almost as if she were a prostitute. This is, then, the first Portuguese film that highlights female sexual freedom and contrasts it to a patriarchal and macho society. Despite its material, it received a subsidy from the Fundo Nacional do Cinema and was passed by the censorship, albeit with a few cuts. The film deals with several themes that were taboo at the time: sexuality, silence, clandestine lives that in the end conceal the death of a black-marketeer. It even contains a rape scene, perhaps the most violent of any in Portuguese cinema of the Estado Novo. But the greatest taboo it broke, taking in all the others, was dealing with censorship itself, the lack of freedom and political persecution.

The director, António da Cunha Telles, indicated that the film had suffered just two cuts: 'During the shooting everyone thought that the film would be banned and have fifty cuts. There had been a change in Portugal, and when the film went to the censors it only had two cuts, one shot showing a shanty town and a cut in the love scene between Marta and the fashion photographer'.[13] However, the censors' report shows that there were later cuts — to do with scenes of violence — imposed over nearly a year, before the film could finally be exhibited.

In fact, the censors' report on the film states that on 27 September 1969 the film was classified as

> for adults over 17 years of age, with the following cuts: a) between the scene 'Boite Relógio' and 'Apartament (letter)', reduce substantially the bedroom scene; b) in scene 52 (leaving the football), cut the image of poor children next to the wooden benches; c) in scene 68 ('Zoological garden'), cut, <u>if it is possible to avoid a jump in the sound</u>, the sentence that starts with 'Sometimes...' and ends in 'obliged to kill'; d) between scene 71 ('Colombo') and the scene 'Azorean woman — death of Victor Lopes', cut the image in which an old woman selling newspapers appears. [censors' own underlining]

On 16 October 1969 it is mentioned that, on checking the cuts, 'they are not done in a satisfactory way. Thus, in that of section a) the scene should be reduced more substantially, which should be done with the moviola.' On 21 August 1970 it says they should make 'the following cuts in the film *O cerco*: a) substantial reduction in the bedroom scene between Marta and her husband; b) suppression of the image of Marta naked, in the mirror, in the "boutique"'. Despite everything, *O cerco* was approved by the censors, probably for the reason expressed here, and evident in the films of the Cinema Novo: it suggests, without referring explicitly.

The theme of adultery and marital crisis will appear more openly in films

---

[13] António da Cunha Telles, in *Écran 72*, 8 (Sept/Oct 1972), p. 65.

of the following decade such as *O passado e o presente* (1971), *Uma abelha na chuva* (1971), *Crime de amor* (1972), *A santa aliança* (1977), etc. Some of them dwell on the very concept of the family, such as *A Sagrada família* (1973), by João César Monteiro, *O mal-amado* (1974), by Fernando Matos Silva, *Brandos costumes* (1974), by Alberto Seixas Santos, and *Sofia e a educação sexual* (1973), by Eduardo Geada. The last three films reflect on the figure of the father as the focus of the family and patriarchal society. *O mal-amado* was the last film to be banned outright, and the first to be seen after the April 1974 revolution. It challenges the submissive role of the housewife faced with a family headed by an oppressive husband and father.

O cerco, the theme of which is women's emancipation, and *O mal-amado*, which tackles the loss of male power, could even be considered feminist films, because, as well as taking a female point of view, they make a diagnosis of the position of women in the Portuguese society of the time, and take their side.

Curiously, the film *Lotação esgotada* (1971), by Manuel de Guimarães, regarded as the Portuguese director closest to neo-realism, was not censored. This can perhaps be explained by the fact that although it alludes clearly enough to the political system, and makes reference to strikes abroad and to the system of denunciations, the main plot of the film focuses on a cemetery — something grotesque enough to distract the attention of the viewer (and of the censors) from possible ideological ambiguities. By veering into satire, the director was able to characterize the society of the time without the film being censored.

In the censors' report, to be found in the Torre do Tombo National Archive, it is stated that on 10 December 1971 *Lotação esgotada* was classified in Group C, i.e. for those aged fourteen and above, with the cuts indicated in the script, and that the film should end before the youngsters leave the cemetery. However, on the 29th of the same month the cuts were all lifted, bar one, which later was also waived. The material on the film is not accompanied by an annotated script, but in the censors' report, under the list of cuts, appears the following in blue pencil, subsequently crossed out: 'as well as the shots of naked breasts.'

Nevertheless, the case of *Lotação esgotada* is surprising, especially as Manuel de Guimarães was considered a leftist director, and his work had previously been extensively cut. For example, at least fourteen minutes of his film *O trigo e o joio* (1964–65) was cut by the censors.[14] *Lotação esgotada*, on the contrary, was subsidised by the Fundo Nacional do Cinema, which leads us to suppose that the relationship between directors and the Comissão de Censura was not straightforward, and undoubtedly involved discussions on matters of common interest.

The film *O recado* (1970–72) also escaped censorship, which can be explained by the changes made to the plot: the director, Fonseca e Costa, decided to 'disguise' the role of an underground activist by 'transforming' a communist

---

[14] Leonor Areal, *Cinema português: um país imaginado*, 2 vols (Lisbon: Edições 70, 2011), I, 319.

into a smuggler.[15] However, certain parts of the film, especially those dealing with criminal activities, leave a visible ambiguity by alluding to clandestinity and police repression. These scenes certainly set tongues wagging, as João Bénard da Costa notes: 'the story of smugglers scarcely disguised (any more than was necessary for the film to pass the censorship) that the struggle was between clandestine activists and agents of the PIDE. The public understood the "secondary meaning" and recognized themselves in their hopes and despairs.'[16]

Of all the cases of film censorship during the time of Marcello Caetano, that of *A promessa* (1972) stands out as one of the most interesting because the file includes a letter of appeal from the director, António de Macedo. On 20 September 1972 the film was classified as 'Group D, with the following cuts: 1) all the dialogue crossed out on pages 17 and 18; 2) the final shot of the naked couple and the chanting of the Benedictus that accompanies it.' The censored material, all crossed through in green pencil, corresponds to the dialogue between a traditionalist priest and a modern young priest, and goes as follows:

> Contrary to what people think religion is a business transaction too. A spiritual one, certainly, but a business transaction, between the human and the divine. [...] Furthermore, it is Christ himself who teaches that. Since he was speaking to Jews, most of his parables tell only stories about money, debts, payments and creditors. Like the parable of the wealthy young man, the parable of the hired workers contracted at a penny each, that of the profitability of the mines, the payment of tribute, the money lost which is found, and which is worth more than all the rest, the parable of the bad steward, and of the debtors, and many more. Well, if Christ is the first to teach, with such insistence, that the Kingdom of Heaven is an immense banking house that pays good interest when there is good capital invested, but that it would expropriate mercilessly those who owe... why be so surprised, Father João, at the self-seeking pledges that our people make?

António de Macedo wrote a letter, dated 12 October 1972, to Dr Caetano de Carvalho, Chairman of the Comissão de Recursos, explaining all of the symbolism of the film in a very laboured way, with the aim, above all, of conveying the importance of retaining the original scheme of the film. On 29 December 1972 the minutes note: 'By higher authority, the film is approved, without cuts, for showing in studios. In other cinemas, it may only be allowed with the cuts indicated. It is also agreed that the images of the second cut (the final scene of the film) may be shown provided that the sound (with the religious chanting) is eliminated.'

The Comissão de Exame e Classificação dos Espectáculos met on 17 October 1972, and its minutes refer to matters that help us to understand the discussion that the film provoked amongst the members of the panel. The Chairman, António Caetano de Carvalho, started by stating that he had seen the film *A*

---

[15] Information provided personally by the Portuguese director António Pedro Vasconcelos, in March 2013.
[16] João Bénard da Costa, *O cinema português nunca existiu* (Lisbon: CTT, 1996), p. 88.

promessa, approved by the Commission, with two cuts, claiming that if he had seen it previously he would have ordered further cuts — cuts which he then detailed, although they are not specified in the minutes. The Chairman then emphasized to the Commission that in cases of doubt, such as that film, and particularly where a Portuguese film was concerned, a working group should not run the risk of making a decision on its own initiative. 'In that way, the desired uniformity of criteria would be prejudiced, as well as creating inconvenient or dangerous precedents, particularly in relation to foreign films.'

The Chairman then reported that the director had appealed against the two cuts imposed by the Commission, 'while noting that the Comissão de Recursos, in examining the material in question, had raised serious doubts with regard to the two images previously mentioned.' He then went on to read out the letter from António de Macedo, who, amongst other things, proposed the release of the film uncut, for exhibition exclusively in studio cinemas in Lisbon and Porto. The minute continues:

> It was underlined by the Chairman that the difficulty with this film went beyond the Commission, and it should not be forgotten that the Administration had certain values to defend. Furthermore, there seems to be not the slightest doubt, in view of the opinion given by this Commission and by that of Resources, not to mention that given unanimously by a group of ten padres for whom the film was specially shown, that the reduced cuts demanded already represent an incontestably benevolent decision, and that decision should therefore not be altered in any way, although that should only be passed on to the interested parties after the matter has been submitted to other proceedings.

Finally, the Chairman recommended to the panel members that 'in future, where there are cases of doubt such as this film, the groups should not make a decision without submitting the problem to the Commission, particularly when dealing with Portuguese films, even if they are works of art, since in such cases the problems always become more difficult.'

From what we can ascertain, this film was one of those that brought the director the most difficulties with censorship.[17] He later admitted that he had made the film in 1972, 'as if there were no censorship in Portugal... (Here in parentheses, there was censorship, and how! It imposed on *Promessa* heavy cuts which I refused to accept, and the battle with that sinister institution was draining and went on for four months until it could be released [...]).'[18] In fact the film was due to be released in October 1973, but the premiere was cancelled, and the impasse continued over four months of bitter negotiations between SEIT, the Direcção do Centro Português de Cinema and the director. Finally,

[17] António de Macedo explains these difficulties in detail in his book *Como se fazia cinema em Portugal: inconfidências de um ex-praticante* (Lisbon: Apenas Livros Ld.ª, 2007), which is available for public reference in the library of the Cinemateca Portuguesa.
[18] António de Macedo, in José de Matos-Cruz, *António de Macedo: cinema, a viragem de uma época* (Lisbon: Publicações Dom Quixote, 2000), p. 32.

in 1974, the Secretary of State gave way, and *A promessa* was approved without cuts, shortly before the 25 April revolution.[19]

Perdido por cem... (1971), by António-Pedro Vasconcelos, escaped virtually uncensored, although one might think that there were grounds for censorship. In fact, the protagonist, Artur, hesitates between remaining in Portugal and leaving the country. At that time, going abroad meant avoiding being called up for military service and sent to fight in the colonial wars in Africa. These reasons are not mentioned explicitly, allowing the film to pass the censors without cuts, but they would have been clearly understood by those seeing the film. The theme of young people without any clear direction in life also appeared in films such as *O cerco* (1969) and *O recado* (1971), followed by *Índia* (1972), *O mal-amado* (1973), *Meus amigos* (1974), and up to *Oxalá* (1980), the second full-length film by António-Pedro Vasconcelos. There were other innovative aspects of *Perdido por cem...*, themselves revealing of a change in the mentality of the Portuguese, which, remarkably, the censors allowed to pass, namely a woman pregnant by an unknown father, the bare breasts of the character Joana, and occasional amorous encounters and behaviour that challenged the traditional notions of what was considered decent up to that time.

The censors' report on the film states that on 29 December 1972 it was classified 'in Group D [over 18 years of age], with the following cuts: a) cut of the images in which Artur and the prostitute appear, from the phrase "I went out into the street", at shot 398, up to the end of the 4th reel (shot 406, inclusive); b) removal of the words 'porra' [damn it] in shot 508, and 'sacana' [crook] in shot 678.' However, on 25 January 1973 it was agreed to allow an appeal 'lifting the cuts for showing in Studio cinemas and maintaining the first cut (scenes with the prostitute) for showing in other outlets.'

The Spanish-Portuguese film *O sinal vermelho* (1973), directed by Rafael R. Marchent, was classified in Group C (over fourteen years of age), although the trailer approved for the same group was censored, 'with the scene showing the drug addicts cut.'

Despite the previously mentioned approach of this generation of filmmakers, of concealment and implication as a way of dealing with political and social topics of the time, some films still failed to escape censorship. This was the case with *Meus amigos* (1973), by António da Cunha Telles, which in a way served as a premonition of the April revolution, alluding in a subtle (or not so subtle) way to the political police, to workers' strikes, and even showing the naked body of the character Helena, when she is just getting out of the bed where she has been lying with Eduardo.

Even so, *Meus amigos* was not banned but it did suffer various cuts: the

---

[19] For a more detailed analysis of *A promessa*, see Ana Bela Morais, 'A Promessa e outros filmes: a censura no Portugal marcelista', *Aniki. Revista Portuguesa da Imagem em Movimento*, 2.2 (2015), 201–19. The journal is published by AIM (Associação de Investigadores da Imagem em Movimento) and available online at <www.aim.org.pt/aniki>.

original version of the film, as presented to the censors, was around three hours long, but it was reduced to 139 minutes. The appeal by the director to the Comissão de Exame e Classificação de Espectáculos was rejected, but it is nevertheless very interesting because it claims that the censorship caused jumps in continuity in the film, in such a way that the public would understand that cuts had been ordered by the censors. In contrast to the customary argument made in appeals, that the film was a work of art, this appeal attempted to argue that the censorship itself would be shown in a bad light if it went ahead with the intended cuts.

The cuts made to the film are all detailed in the censors' report. On 15 February 1974, the film was classified

> In Group D [over 18 years of age], on the following terms: a) suppression of the images corresponding to the words in the text marked in blue pencil, in shots 2, 3 [1 — Mate, that guy... those guys there from the police... from the force... 2 — special... 3 — special, isn't he? [...]], 7 [[...] and I would say that in the end the... the executioner at Anselwitz [sic] wasn't to blame either, was he?... because... everyone does their job] and 549 ['You're kidding me?... mate...this, mate, it's a... sub-agency, mate, of the American gang, mate. France too, it's the same thing... the same filth from all the countries where I was... <u>It's just here, it smells much worse... and it's much worse for your heart...</u>' — all this scene is enclosed in a rectangle of blue pencil, and the part underlined corresponds to a further blue rectangle]; b) suppression of the images corresponding to scenes 647 to 684 inclusive [dialogue that employs the metaphor of mice that are obliged in laboratory experiments to move on a green light, if they go on red they get electric shocks, while amber indicates a transgression — much the same as happens with the characters or people who disobey the social and political rules of the Caetano regime], 744 [We have to take possession of private property.], 807 [806 — The capitalists... are... 807 — they have their riflemen...], 3089, 3090 [3089 — Christ the King [statue in Lisbon]. 3090 — We're killing Christ the King. Wait there, wait there...], 4014 to 4019 inclusive [A character asks what monument is that he's looking at and the another replies: 'it's the ugly face of Portugal'], 4029 [Grr.. grr... the Church, mate! Grr... Grr...], 4373 [You're right, mate... This, it's all rotten. We ought to bring it all down.], 4517 and 4518 [4517 — You need to be on the inside of things. You need disciplined action. On the margins you can't achieve anything. I came back because I wanted to. 4518 — Yes, by revolution, from the inside, isn't it?].

As we can see, all the dialogues and images that were ordered removed from the film correspond to references to the lack of freedom in the country, to the political police, and to the need for revolution, as well as making criticisms of religion.

On 21 February 1974 the Comissão de Recursos refused to grant the director's appeal: 'upholding the decision that was appealed, that is, keeping all the cuts indicated.' On 9 March 1974 it is noted that

> there should also be suppressed the images corresponding to scenes 704 to

710 [704 — The Portuguese are there, because... they were deported. 705 — The Portuguese were there because monopoly capitalism... 706 — They were deported there... 707 — ... in fact he made a great leap forward, and this gang had the opportunity to reach a labour market, it was... it was an open door was created and it was created because there was a big step forward, that is to say... 708 — I think you should keep your voices down... 709 — down? 710 — uh-huh...], inclusive, which by a slip that we much regret, were not indicated in the communication mentioned [that of February].

Another film that was censored was *Malteses, burgeses e às vezes...* (1972–74), by Artur Semedo. Using a new type of satire, the film is able to introduce a series of jokes that touch on political matters, but without ever putting into question the political system itself, or even alluding to the colonial wars. The fact that the film was shot almost entirely in Angola and had its first showing there before coming to Lisbon may have facilitated its acceptance in mainland Portugal. Even so, it was still censored. As is mentioned in the censors' report dated 26 March 1974, the film was classified as 'Group D, with a reduction in the "striptease" sequence, which will affect the final scenes, on page 4, and the suppression of the images of the naked couple by the shower, also on page 4. The *Trailer* is approved for the same group, with a cut to the image referred to in point b), relating to the film.'

Malteses, burgueses e às vezes... made use of the greater freedom in matters of sexuality, customs and forms of address that were permitted by the censors in Angola in order to criticize the restrictions inherent to metropolitan life. This is also the only Portuguese film to allude, in its prologue, to the massive emigration by Portuguese to Europe.

As to films that were first censored but then approved without cuts, we noted two: *Lotação esgotada* and *A promessa. O recado*, which seemingly could have been censored, was not. The films that were censored number five in all: *O cerco, Perdido por cem..., O sinal vermelho, Meus amigos* and *Malteses, burgueses e às vezes...*

As we can see, the way in which each film was evaluated by the censors was not always consistent, which leads us to believe that the Comissão de Censura was not governed by rigid rules; rather, each film was evaluated by the criteria of those serving on the board of censors at the time, or even by a particular censor. The subjectivity inherent in the system of censorship in Portugal is also obvious in the case of those films that were banned outright, as we shall see below.

Portuguese Films That Were Banned, or Nearly

Apart from the Portuguese films censored, some were banned outright. As stated in the introduction, although the censorship of films softened noticeably during the period of the so-called 'Marcellist spring', between late 1968 and 1970, from the latter date the Comissão de Censura become once again narrower and more rigorous in its criteria.

As Lauro António mentions, referring to Portuguese and foreign cinema,

> on 9 December 1970, a statement by the Union of Entertainment Guilds, signed by Engineer José Gilera, was delivered to Marcello Caetano. An 'alarming' text that detailed a change of direction in the criteria for censorship: of 157 films censored and intended for the first months of the 1970/71 season, 34 (21.6%) were banned, with 76 (49.7%) being subjected to mutilation![20]

Before the April 1974 revolution, the only Portuguese film passed that addressed the issue of the wars in Africa was *29 irmãos* (1964-65), by Augusto Fraga. This may have been due to the political alignment of the director, since the film, despite praising the soldiers' sacrifices in the name of patriotism, nevertheless alluded to their suffering, as well as the fact that many died there — something that not even the press were allowed to do, as has been convincingly demonstrated by Cândido de Azevedo.[21]

Some allude very vaguely to the issue of war, such *Mudar de vida* (1966), by Paulo Rocha, and *A promessa* (1972), by António de Macedo. Films that referred more directly to the wars were banned, namely *Índia* (1972), by António Faria, and *O mal-amado* (1973), by Fernando Matos Silva.

In fact, two phenomena were almost completely hidden from Portuguese cinema during Marcello Caetano's time: the wars in Africa and mass emigration. Only a French film, *O salto* (1967), by Christian de Chalonge, raised the latter subject, with its plot centred on clandestine Portuguese emigration to France. Emigration is also shown peripherally in the film *Malteses, burgueses e às vezes...* (1973), by Artur Semedo, mentioned above. The prologue is made up of documentary footage of emigrants leaving on a train, while later we see the people-smugglers making deals at the frontier town of Vilar Formoso. The rest of the film, contrary to expectations, takes place in Angola. Other very brief references to the theme of emigration can be seen in *Os verdes anos* (1963) and *Mudar de vida* (1965), both by Paulo Rocha, *Perdido por cem* (1971-73), by António-Pedro Vasconcelos, and *A promessa* (1972), by António de Macedo. After *O salto*, many films referred to emigrants, but telling of their return to Portugal, and not their departure.

It is surprising that *O salto* was neither banned nor censored, being premiered in a studio cinema in Lisbon.[22] This can be explained by the 'Marcellist spring', but also by the fact that it was politically inoffensive. Despite

---

[20] Lauro António, *Cinema e censura em Portugal*, 2nd edn (Lisbon: Biblioteca Museu República e Resistência, 2001), p. 49.

[21] Cândido de Azevedo, *Mutiladas e proibidas: para a história da censura literária em Portugal nos tempos do Estado Novo* (Lisbon: Editorial Caminho, 1997).

[22] As mentioned above, during the Caetano period it was common for films to be premiered in studio cinemas, patronized by audiences considered cultured and therefore sufficiently educated to be able to understand the films being shown there.

showing clandestine emigration and the motivations behind it, it also showed that emigrants met with great hardships abroad, very often much worse than if they had remained in Portugal.

Hence only two ideologically contrasting films, *O salto* and *29 irmãos*, refer directly to these two tragic themes. The social and cultural silence to be found in the remaining films of the time can be explained by self-censorship on the part of directors, driven by their desire to avoid the cutting or banning of their works.

As mentioned above, the directors of Portuguese New Cinema did not attempt to produce films of political resistance. As Eduardo Geada notes: 'a cinema of resistance, in the true acceptance of the term, demands a subordination of the aesthetic point of view to the political point of view. And in that respect, very little was done.'[23] It might perhaps be said that there was an active cinema of resistance in the early 1970s, particularly amongst the banned films, such as Geada's first film, *Sofia e a educação sexual* (1973).

Furthermore, there were films that were not officially banned by the censors, but which could nevertheless not be exhibited. This was the case with *Grande, grande era a cidade* (1971), by Rogério Ceitil, which was shown at the II Santarém Film Festival and then immediately banned by the censors, and 'other films were known which could not be shown in Portuguese cinemas, despite not being formally banned, [such as] João César Monteiro's *Quem espera por sapatos de defunto morre descalço*'.[24]

This short, shot between 1969 and 1970, was one of the films supported by the Calouste Gulbenkian Foundation, through the intermediary of the Centro Português de Cinema, but 'there were problems with the censors, who cut dialogue and references to "Admiral Salads", an obvious allusion to the then President of the Republic. César always refused to show the film with the cuts.'[25] The film was shown only in 1979, on the RTP 2 television channel. The short film *Jaime* (1973), by António Reis, also produced by the Centro Português de Cinema, 'surprisingly, was also banned, perhaps because they did not want people to see what a mental hospital looked like in Marcelo's Portugal.'[26]

Another film banned by the censors, shot in Mozambique, was *Deixem-me ao menos subir às palmeiras* (1971), by Lopes Barbosa. The documentary *Esplendor selvagem* (1957–72), by António de Sousa, shot in Angola, got a screening in Mozambique, but was considered 'anti-political' by the Angola censors. The minutes of the censors' meeting that discussed *Esplendor selvagem*, dated 12 June 1973, suggest that the producer should make the cuts indicated and add a subtitle, implying perhaps that the film could then be approved. However, for its meeting of 31 July 1973, the minutes state:

[23] Eduardo Geada, *O imperialismo e o fascismo no cinema* (Lisbon: Moraes Editora, 1977), p. 93.
[24] Lauro António, *Cinema e censura em Portugal*, p. 31.
[25] João Bénard da Costa, *Cinema português, anos Gulbenkian* (Lisbon: Gulbenkian Foundation, 2007), p. 27.
[26] Bénard da Costa, *Cinema português, anos Gulbenkian*, p. 35.

Moving on to the cases for cinema, Senhor Dr. José Cabral stated that, having examined again the supposedly new version of the film *Esplendor selvagem*, he came to the conclusion that it was practically the same as the earlier film, with all the problems then found by the Commission. Having read the official note received from the Overseas Ministry, with an unfavourable view based on the opinion given by the delegates who attended the special showing, the Commission, after an exchange of relevant impressions, decided to reject the said film for the commercial circuit.

The film *Nem amantes, nem amigos* (1968), by Orlando Vitorino, was also banned by the censors. And *Nojo aos cães* (1970), by António de Macedo, undoubtedly the most iconoclastic and experimental film made in those years, was bound to be banned, showing as it did young people in rebellion against the regime, out of control, and referring to the youth revolts that were taking place at the time in America and France.

Índia (1972), by António Faria, openly anti-regime in its content, was never even submitted to the censors. As the director states:

> After the film was finished, when we were innocently thinking about its public showing, which would have to pass the prior censorship of the Comissão de Censura, we learned of its imminent seizure and the destruction of the negative. [...] And so this film and others were taken clandestinely out of the country, in 1973.[27]

This film was shown only in February 1975.

A sagrada família (1972), by João César Monteiro — perhaps the most provocative film of the period, because it challenged and destroyed any conventional view of the family — was another film that was never even banned, because its director, after the cuts made to *Quem espera por sapatos de defunto morre descalço*, never submitted it to the censors.

The second film by Rogério Ceitil, *Cartas na mesa* (1973-75), practically a documentary on the period after the death of Salazar and the influences of May '68, was also banned, along with Eduardo Geada's *Sofia e a educação sexual* (1973-74). The latter is hardly surprising, since never up to then, and very rarely afterwards even, had the subject of female desire been tackled by Portuguese cinema. The director, however, affects not to understand why his film has been banned:

> Despite the subject of the film being unprecedented in the field of Portuguese cinema, and daring, as was said at the time, I had deliberately conceived the staging and planning exactly on the basis of a mechanism of repression, censorship, that is, permitted by the ontology of the cinematic image: everything that was capable of upsetting the puritanism of the official censorship, I innocently thought, was out of the field of view. What was visible in the framing and the editing of the film referred systematically to what was invisible and which only the imagination of the viewer could

[27] António Faria, 'Ficção e Guerra Colonial: um filme', in *A Guerra Colonial: realidade e ficção. Actas do I Congresso Internacional* (Lisbon: Ed. Notícias, 2001), p. 485.

complete, as he liked. The hypocrisy of the ruling morality was precisely one of the subjects of the film, and it seemed to me that, apart from the pragmatic matters of its exhibition, that this aesthetic process was most appropriate for the project.[28]

Sofia e a educação sexual premiered in Lisbon on 1 October 1974 and was an enormous box-office success.

In concluding this section on films banned outright, we find *O mal-amado* (1972), by Fernando Matos Silva. As I mentioned above, this was the last Portuguese film to be banned by the Estado Novo and the first to be allowed after the 25 April revolution. The case papers show that it was banned on 20 February 1974.

Also in the National Archive are the minutes of the Comissão de Censura dated 28 March 1974. They are interesting because they detail the discussion provoked by the film *O mal-amado*, as can be seen from the views given by the censors:

> Senhor Dr. Gonçalves Pereira considered the film very hard to approve, despite a series of cinema critics having classified it as being the best Portuguese film produced to date. However, the optic through which the central character of the film — an oppositionist — sees all the features of Portuguese life (in part true, in part completely distorted), presents an ensemble that, in his view, did not allow the approval of the film, especially given the certainty that, going down the road of making cuts, these would be so numerous that little or nothing comprehensible would be left. Senhor Dr. Gonçalves Pereira also emphasized that the whole part dealing with the soldiers was a very profound attack on the war in Africa, being, therefore, an *a priori* rejection. Bearing in mind that all the criticism in the film took the most negative angle possible, and that in the case of cuts being imposed they would make the film incomprehensible, he concluded by giving the view that within the present criteria of the Commission there was no scope for the approval of the film in question.

Speaking next, Senhor Dr. José Alves Cortês agreed that the Commission's decision was obvious, taking into account the many implications of a political and social nature contained in the film: 'for him, as with the others, the mischief in this film lay particularly in the dialogue in which certain aspects of Portuguese life were enthusiastically criticized, as in the case, for example, of the exaggeration of the ridiculous and the artificial in presenting the middle-class family.' The next censor, Senhor Dr. Quartin Graça, admitted it was not easy to reject the film *in limine*. However, given that the cuts necessary for approval would leave the film incomprehensible, he judged rejection preferable. In effect — he emphasized — there was in the film such a great weight of unacceptable material at the moment, the most serious related to military, political and social aspects, which, in his opinion, would imply a substantial reduction in the film, whether in footage or in sense. Seeing, though, that political and social

[28] Interview with Eduardo Geada in César Príncipe, *A censura de Salazar e Marcelo Caetano*, p. 235.

implications of non-military elements were less serious than those related to the war overseas, he was willing to consider a possible evaluation of the film with all the necessary cuts made.

Senhor Ferreira de Almeida then drew attention to the dangers of showing such a film abroad:

> [...] in his opinion, the case of this film took on an extraordinary seriousness, whatever the findings of the Commission. For his part, he considered it the most difficult case to date, after five years of service on the Commission, that he had been asked to decide upon. On the one hand, the fact of there being under consideration a Portuguese film, involving the investment of important backers — a fact that necessitated careful consideration. And on the other hand, the danger that these films represented for our country and regarding which there had more than once been objections in this Commission. This, and others like it, were films that, if banned in Portugal, would in the end be shown abroad as real weapons against us. For this reason alone he still regretted that, contrary to what he had suggested but had been covered by the Cinema Law, the Secretary of State could not prevent the export of such films. In the present circumstances, the film, if it were shown in Cannes, for example, would be a box-office success, at the expense of the implications of a political kind it involved, of the Brechtianism contained in certain passages, and of the malicious and negative criticism it makes of our military policy. In his view, there were fewer risks in the exhibition of this film in Portugal than in its being showing abroad. Apart from the military aspect related to our struggle in the overseas territories, in which all the implications of the film required complete cutting, he had still no clear position as to whether the film should be approved or rejected. For an informed decision he would need to know from the Instituto Português de Cinema its intentions regarding the release of the film abroad, since clearly once exported it would be used by enemies of our country as an element of propaganda amongst our emigrants. In these circumstances he would adjust his vote according to the criterion to be adopted, that is: if the export of the film was not authorized he would ban it; if the intention was to allow it to leave, then he would approve it, with the cuts to the military part dealing with our struggle in the defence of the overseas territories. [...]

The opinion of the final censor summarized the problem the Commission faced in approving a film like O mal-amado, underlining, albeit indirectly, the moralizing, paternalistic and educational mission with which the Commission was charged:

> Dealing, then, directly with the material of the appeal, [Senhor Dr. João Silva] gave the opinion that as regards the images the film posed no problem apart from the scene in which the woman undresses. The fundamental problem lay, without doubt, in the dialogue, where, between one truth or other, there were passages that cause the gravest misgivings and were worse than poison. Comparing the society to which the film is addressed with what happens to the human body and the effects that a wound provokes in it, and whether it is treated or not, he emphasized that, in the same way, if a

wound is opened up in society (provoked by films like this, by intellectuals, by artists — when they aim their 'works' outwards) and if, from this wound, there is no one to drain the pus to heal it, then it's absolutely certain that in no time at all the infection will spread and turn into leprosy and death. It was this process of disinfection that, with regard to the cinema, has to be exercised by the censors, to combat the danger that if one is passed today, tomorrow it will be another film of the same kind, and in no time they will all be infected. Exactly because he understood that this is a film capable of infecting society he turned it down. [...] In these terms, the Commission decided to refuse the appeal, upholding therefore the rejection of the film *O mal-amado*.

The analogy of an infection that the last member of the panel makes, so vividly described, would certainly have been censored if it had appeared in the dialogue of a film...

So the films that were wholly suppressed in those years (late 1968 to 1974) were as follows: two shorts, *Quem espera por sapatos de defunto morre descalço* and *Jaime*; two films that were never submitted to the censors, *Índia* and *A sagrada família*, and eight other films banned outright, *Nem amantes, nem amigos, Nojo aos cães, Grande, grande era a cidade, Deixam-me ao menos subir às palmeiras, Esplendor selvagem, Cartas na mesa, Sofia e a educação sexual* and *O mal-amado*.

Final Remarks

As I have demonstrated, despite a slight relaxation in the criteria for censorship of Portuguese and foreign films — although in this study the focus has been on the former — in the early Caetano years (late 1968 to 1970) this relaxation was largely illusory, and short-lived. The numbers demonstrate this for Portuguese films; those censored or banned were as listed at the end of the last two sections.

As for the criteria of the Comissão de Censura, they varied over the decades, in line with political convenience. As Lauro António remarks: 'pacifist films were banned after 1961. With the country at war pacifism was "unacceptable". And various works of an openly warlike kind were approved for relatively young audiences, as preparation for the war.'[29]

The topics that most concerned the censors had to do mostly with morals and the family, sexual relationships, and behaviour considered disgraceful, such as adultery and abortion. Although with time some expression of sexuality was permitted, they continued to cut images of naked bodies and sensuous representations.

However, over the course of the Caetano period references to the political regime and colonial wars were not permitted, as we have shown above. The

---

[29] António, *Cinema e censura em Portugal*, p. 57.

pressure on the regime seems in fact to have led to a reinforcement of censorship, in an ever more vain attempt to control what was said and shown.

Being products of self-censorship, resulting from a lack of freedom of expression at various levels, the Portuguese films studied here show, by omission, what it was the regime wanted to conceal. That is, by examining what was cut or banned by the censors we can work out what it was that they did not want seen or heard. Even as they follow the values of the regime, films end up being more constrained than the reality they represent, because they project too exactly the required duties, conducts, and moral values. In this way the films are a reflection of the ideology that dominated the cultural and social environment in the Portugal of the time.

Some films, though not censored or banned, show some signs of new times. The plot of the comedy *A maluquinha de Arroios* (1969),[30] by Henrique Campos, full of misunderstandings and infidelities, sketches out the social situation of the time. In the opening scenes it shows youngsters dancing rock'n'roll at a filling station and it even has a *hippy* character. The same happens in *Derrapagem* (1971), the last film by Constantino Esteves, which reflects in a very conventional and moralistic way upon the instability of modern marriages. However, despite its moral leanings, the film still shows the personal dramas of the husband, divided between his marital duty and sexual freedom, as well as the day-dreams of the wife, which make her forget her family commitments. It's interesting to note that films like *A maluquinha de Arroios* and directors like Constatino Esteves are in the antipodes of Cinema Novo and its 'auteurs'.

Portuguese films of this period dealing with national history showed as much as could be said and shown, and, in the cases of the banned films, what was forbidden. After the revolution of 25 April 1974 there would appear a plethora of documentary and contemporary films that tried to say what had until then been forbidden.

Translated from Portuguese by Richard Correll

---

[30] An updating of the stage play by André Brun, first performed in 1916.

Reviews

RHIAN ATKIN, *Lisbon Revisited: Urban Masculinities in Twentieth-Century Portuguese Fiction* (Oxford: Legenda, 2014). 196 pages. Print.

Reviewed by SÍLVIA OLIVEIRA (Rhode Island College)

Lisbon Revisited is a study 'about men and masculinities' in a society where, according to the author, Rhian Atkin, 'empirical studies of gendered behaviours' are lacking (p. 1). This monograph merges the trendy fields of urban studies, masculinities and modernity studies, and politically engaged literature through analysis of the works of two of the most prominent Portuguese writers of the twentieth century, Fernando Pessoa and José Saramago, and the Portuguese author, Luís de Sttau Monteiro. Atkin's work is offered as a testimony to literature bearing 'the marks of social and cultural realities' (p. 1) that allow for a deeper understanding of aspects of Portuguese society in the twentieth century, suggesting a re-visioning of European accounts of literary modernism (gendered, political and urban). The title's allusion to 'revisiting' weds the celebrated poem by Fernando Pessoa's heteronym, Álvaro de Campos, 'Lisbon Revisited', and the famed historical revisionist impulse in Saramago's novel, *The History of the Siege of Lisbon*, providing an appropriate reference to methodology.

Atkin clarifies from the onset that the number of Portuguese writers who focused on life experience in Lisbon in the twentieth century is significant and notable, and therefore the selections from Pessoa, Saramago and Sttau Monteiro are meant to 'approach canonical or semi-canonical authors from a new angle [...] [recuperating] the provocative originality of these texts' (p. 3). Works selected are *Livro do Desassossego* [*Book of Disquiet*], by Fernando Pessoa/Bernardo Soares, written between 1929 and 1935 and first published in 1982; *Um Homem não Chora* [*A Man Doesn't Cry* — untranslated] by Luís de Sttau Monteiro of 1960; *História do Cerco de Lisboa* [*The History of the Siege of Lisbon*] by José Saramago of 1989.

Of the three, Pessoa and Saramago are the canonical authors and subjects of distinguished scholarship in British academia. Luís de Sttau Monteiro, on the other hand, is one of many sidelined and censored authors whose work throughout the 1960s contributed to the intellectual and political pool of resistance to the Salazar regime. Sttau Monteiro was also the son of a Portuguese diplomat and lived in London for a time during the 1940s. This connection to British culture and society is relevant for studying his work and Atkin links it to the 'Angry Young Men' phenomenon in the UK. Moreover, Luís de Sttau

Monteiro is currently enjoying a reappraisal in Portugal, notably since his play, *Felizmente Há Luar!* [*Thankfully There is Moonlight!*] (1961) was included in the official high school curriculum of readings on twentieth-century Portuguese literature. Rhian Atkin's contribution to the understanding of this seldom studied Portuguese author is both important and timely.

The four chapters of *Lisbon Revisited* titled 'Masculine Subjectivities in the Modern City', 'Masculinities in the Streets', 'Masculinities and Consumer Society', 'Men at Home, Men at Work' include a comparative analysis between the three books (by Soares, Saramago and Sttau Monteiro) from a multi-disciplinary perspective. Reading Sttau Monteiro along with Pessoa and Saramago in a time span that covers some of the most significant socio-political and literary changes that occurred in Portugal during the twentieth century brings fresh insight to *Lisbon Revisited*. The skilful *close cultural reading* of these three Portuguese authors and the three books selected is relevant to all specialists and readers of Portuguese literature and urban masculinities studies.

OLIVIA SHERINGHAM, *Transnational Religious Spaces: Faith and the Brazilian Migration Experience*, Migration, Diasporas and Citizenship Series (Basingstoke and New York: Palgrave Macmillan, 2013). 226 pages. Print, ebook.

Reviewed by ALAN P. MARCUS (Towson University, MD)

The book includes seven chapters, an appendix (with a list of research participants), notes, bibliography and index. There are six figures and two tables. Dr Olivia Sheringham has focused on Brazilian migrants in London on two levels: by examining the broader processes of global transformation, and the ways in which immigrants adapt to such processes.

This book is a much-needed scholarly publication, and despite the fact that Brazilians have had a long history of relations with the UK (ranging from economic and diplomatic relations to exiles and, more recently, immigrants), scholars have been slow to look at Brazilian immigrants in the UK, with little research available until now. In this case, I would have chosen 'in England' (or more specifically, perhaps, 'in London') at the end of the book title.

Sheringham provides a cohesive transnational theoretical backdrop which sets the context for excerpts from narratives of migrants' interviews she conducted, and which she effectively uses to highlight her statements. She also includes useful excerpts from her own field notes. By drawing on migrants' narratives, she reveals how religion cannot be confined to one place; rather it influences those who experience both the absence of family or friends, and the lives of those who themselves migrate.

Sheringham's research was conducted in London and Brazil between 2009 and 2010. She traces the relationship between religion and globalization on multiple scales, pointing out that Brazil is the second largest Protestant country in the world and the largest Pentecostal, and also the world capital of Spiritism (Kardecism). Here she traces the three main currents of Protestantism in Brazil to early twentieth century, then 'conversion Protestantism' which originated in US Protestant Revivalism, and, lastly to Neo-Pentecostalism, which has emerged recently and which is characterized by the 'Theology of Prosperity'. She makes the important point that there is no separation between before/after Brazil/London; rather they are interconnected transnational religious spaces. Moreover, Brazilian immigrants in the UK do not fit neatly into the dichotomy of 'local' and 'global'. She is interested in how Brazilian immigrants negotiate their religious beliefs and how they create new connections between different practices in different places and, what they 'do' with religion. She aptly explains to the reader how religion is 'practiced, experienced, imagined and embodied by migrants as they create and inhabit spaces that span multiple scales' (p. 7).

Religious remittances is a concept she explores commendably. Sheringham found common patterns of downward mobility among migrants, and that Brazilians are most likely to be irregular in their legal status. She underscored current threads in her research, which include how the church became 'family' (the church as a refuge); a search for a sense of belonging (religious community or immigrant); that faith was a way to suppress *saudades* (a Portuguese word for 'homesickness'); that returning to Brazil presented a further challenge of re-adaptation; and, lastly, that religious remittances play an important role in the return context as well as in the migration process. She argues that economic reasons should not mask multiple and inter-related decisions to migrate including the role of religion — which she makes convincingly. She concludes that transnational religious spaces are exclusionary as much as they are inclusionary.

Sheringham effectively and skilfully reveals the interplay between religion and transnationalism. This is a well-researched book with excellent sources. This book is a must-read for all levels of diaspora and immigrant students and scholars.

ANA CLAUDIA SURIANI DA SILVA and SANDRA GUARDINI VASCONCELLOS (eds), *Books and Periodicals in Brazil 1768–1930: A Transatlantic Perspective* (Oxford: Legenda, 2014). 294 pages. Print.

Reviewed by ORNA LEVIN (Unicamp, Brazil)

Although many essays been written about the expansion of the British book market and the corresponding increase in readership during the nineteenth century, British transatlantic exchanges have usually been considered within the framework of the English-speaking world, to the exclusion of Brazil.

Recent studies, however, suggest that after the Portuguese court moved to Rio de Janeiro, in 1808, as a result of the Napoleonic invasion of southern Europe, the British traders and European commercial agents who followed did more than simply settle there, introducing new cultural patterns that affected various aspects of daily life and providing local people with new political references and liberal ideas. This new collection of essays recently published by Legenda, which has the suggestive title of *Books and Periodicals in Brazil, 1768–1930: A Transatlantic Perspective*, edited by Ana Cláudia Suriani, Lecturer in the School of European Languages, Culture and Society, University College London, and Sandra Vasconcelos, Lecturer in English Literature at the University of São Paulo, should help to overcome the lack of familiarity on the part of European readers with topics relating to this aspect of Brazil's place in international book history.

The thirteen essays included in the publication will help readers better understand how the advance in printing techniques and the publishing trade contributed to a larger circulation of books, magazines and musical scores, among other forms of printed production. In particular, they turn our attention to less evident issues behind the editorial enterprises, which were run mainly by British, Portuguese and French dealers.

The chapters encourage a deep analysis of the cultural transference that was made possible, to a large extent, by the increasing availability of foreign titles for reading. Foreign periodicals, such as the *Edinburgh Review, Monthly Magazine, Blackwood's Magazine, Revue Britannique* and *Journal de Débats*, along with a variety of fictional and non-fictional books, provided readers with a constant source of information. They also provided a literary model for local editors to launch Brazilian periodicals. Furthermore, the practice of importing printed matter gave a stimulus to the birth of a national literature.

The lack of international agreements on copyright enabled the free borrowing of material as well as unauthorized translations and other appropriations of texts, while adaptations and local versions of foreign creations lay behind the founding of a Brazilian national literature. The examination in this book of the long process of cultural transference of commodities, practices and ideas points not only to the demand for reading materials that led to the opening of foreign bookstores and the installation of reading rooms and membership associations, such as the British Circulating Library, but also to the way in which local readers and writers, inspired by nationalist sentiments, reacted to the constant exposure to European printed materials. Examples of their impact are the regulation of intellectual property, put into effect later in the nineteenth century, and the growing pressures for writing to be accepted and organized as a profession.

The spread of print journalism and other printed materials around European countries and their colonies in the nineteenth century benefited from a modern transportation systems, such as the British railway companies and the transatlantic steamships lines that connected Liverpool, Le Havre and Bordeaux with Brazilian ports. Equally, the transmission of news was facilitated by the extension of the telegraphic networks in association with the British construction companies, and with the inauguration of transatlantic cable services, which shortened the lines of communications between Europe and Brazil. By analysing the birth of Brazilian literary and journalistic creations modelled on European patterns these essays explain a lot about the preferences of readers for novels, their taste for certain literary images or for fashion patterns, as well as for revolutionary political ideas.

This is a collection of original studies that makes for interesting reading.

Abstracts

The Redactor of the Second Version of the 'Chronicle of 1344': Initial Traits for the Drawing up of a 'Facial Composite'

ISABEL DE BARROS DIAS

ABSTRACT. This article outlines some potential features of the profile of the redactor of the second version of the *Chronicle of 1344*. After a presentation of the state of the art, three thematic lines are referred to. These trends are evident in certain passages of the text, suggesting that such characteristics could be attributable to its author's preferences: a clerical penchant akin to the Franciscan models; a didactic trend, in line with *specula principorum*; and a taste for *topoi* and expressions similar to those used in courtly literature.

KEYWORDS. *Crónica de 1344* (2nd version), author, Franciscan, *specula*, chivalric novel.

RESUMO. Artigo onde são esboçados alguns traços do que poderá ser o perfil do redactor da segunda versão da *Crónica de 1344*. Depois de uma apresentação do estado da arte, são referidas três linhas temáticas acentuadas em algumas passagens do texto, o que permite sugerir que se trate de características atribuíveis a preferências deste autor: um pendor clerical próximo dos modelos franciscanos; uma tendência didática próxima da linha dos *specula principorum*; e o gosto por *topoi* e expressões semelhantes aos usados na literatura cortês.

PALAVRAS-CHAVE. *Crónica de 1344* (2ª redação), autor, franciscano, *specula*, romance de cavalaria.

The Subversion of Hate Literature in Anrique da Mota's 'Farce of the Tailor'

ANNA MATHESON

ABSTRACT. Written within a decade of the 1497 general conversion of the Jews in Portugal, Anrique da Mota's *Farce of the Tailor* appears, at first glance, to be an overt satire deriding a New Christian: Mota uses the common dramatic form of the mock trial to pass judgement on the religious sincerity of a Jew who was baptized voluntarily. In this article, I will show that, despite its clear tone of condemnation and its comic presentation of the convert, the farce is in fact a very serious polemic on the subject of apostasy that highlights the shame and alienation experienced by voluntary converts, scorned by both the Portuguese Old Christians and those who were baptized by force. As shall be made clear, Mota's text presents an implicit yet brazen critique of Manueline policy concerning the Jews that has not hitherto been adequately recognized.

KEYWORDS. Forced conversion, Anrique da Mota, *A Farsa do Alfaiate*, early modern Portugal, Portuguese drama, New Christians, apostasy, Jews.

RESUMO. À primeira vista, a *A Farsa do Alfaiate* que escreveu Anrique da Mota na década seguinte à conversão geral dos judeus de Portugal de 1479, aparenta ser uma sátira ridicularizando abertamente um cristão novo. Mota adota o formato dramático corrente de um processo dramatizado para exprimir seu juízo de valor sobre a sinceridade de um judeu que se faz batizar voluntariamente. O presente artigo busca demonstrar que, indo além do tom de reprovação e da caracterização cómica do personagem, a *Farsa* constitui de fato uma polémica sobre a questão da apostasia, ressaltando a vergonha e o senso de alienação vividos pelos convertidos voluntários, que são achincalhados tanto pelos cristãos velhos de Portugal como por aqueles que são convertidos à força. O artigo também esclarece que, apesar de ainda não estar apropriadamente estabelecido na literatura, o texto de Mota representa uma crítica velada porém destemida à política Manuelina quanto aos judeus.

PALAVRAS-CHAVE. Conversão forçada, Anrique da Mota, *A Farsa do Alfaiate*, drama português, Cristãos Novos, apostasia, Judeus.

A Newly Discovered Novel and its Transnational Author: 'Maria Severn' by Francisca Wood

CLÁUDIA PAZOS ALONSO

ABSTRACT. This article focuses on a transnational Portuguese woman of letters, Francisca Wood, and her novel *Maria Severn* (1869), initially serialized in the pioneering weekly periodical that she directed, *A Voz Feminina*, later renamed *O Progresso* (1868–69). It draws on preliminary archival research to provide new biographical information on Wood, which sheds fresh light on her progressive convictions and British connections. Using as source text what appears to be the only surviving copy of *Maria Severn* in book form — recently discovered in the British Library — I examine the role of Wood as cultural mediator and suggest that the incontrovertible originality of her novel may stem from her creative assimilation of Jane Austen, Elizabeth Gaskell and George Eliot.

KEYWORDS. Periodical press, nineteenth-century novel, Francisca Wood, feminism, Anglo-Portuguese cultural relations, George Eliot.

RESUMO. Este artigo debruça-se sobre uma mulher de letras cosmopolita, Francisca Wood, e o seu romance *Maria Severn* (1869), inicialmente publicado em folhetim no periódico semanal pioneiro de que Wood era diretora, *A Voz Feminina*, cujo nome foi posteriormente alterado para *O Progresso* (1868–69). Esta investigação (ainda em curso) faculta-nos novos dados biográficos sobre Wood, que comprovam as suas convicções, assumidamente progressistas, e os seus contactos em Inglaterra. Usando como fonte o único exemplar atualmente conhecido deste romance em formato livro — recentemente descoberto na

British Library — pretende-se aferir o papel de Wood como mediadora cultural e sugerir que a originalidade incontornável de *Maria Severn* poderá resultar da assimilação criativa que Wood fez de Jane Austen, Elizabeth Gaskell e George Eliot.

PALAVRAS-CHAVE. Imprensa periódica, romance do século XIX, Francisca Wood, feminismo, relações culturais anglo-portuguesas, George Eliot.

Undone Anatomies: Femininity, Performativity and Parody in Mário de Sá-Carneiro's 'A Confissão de Lúcio'

ELEANOR K. JONES

ABSTRACT. 2014 marked the centenary of the publication of Mário de Sá-Carneiro's novel *A Confissão de Lúcio*, a text defined by its complex articulations of sexuality, jealousy and madness. While traditional analyses of the text underplayed the importance of sexuality and eroticism to the plot, more recent readings have revisited the novel to engage with the latent sexual tension between the novel's male protagonists. Sá-Carneiro's use of sexuality and gender as articulated through his two female characters, however, remains overlooked. This study explores the radical possibilities of these intriguing characters, using Judith Butler's poststructuralist theorization of gender and sexual categories to provide a starting point for the development of new perspectives on Sá-Carneiro's classic text.

KEYWORDS. Portugal, Sá-Carneiro, modernism, gender, sexuality, poststructuralism.

RESUMO. O ano de 2014 marcou o centenário da publicação do romance *A Confissão de Lúcio* por Mário de Sá-Carneiro, texto que se caracteriza pelas suas complexas articulações de sexualidade, loucura, e ciúme. Enquanto as análises tradicionais minimizaram a importância de sexualidade e erotismo em relação ao romance, algumas interpretações mais recentes revisaram-no para engajar com a tensão erótica latente entre os seus dois protagonistas masculinos. Contudo, os papéis das personagens femininas na articulação de sexualidade e género do romance ainda não foram investigados. Este artigo utiliza as teorizações pós-estruturalistas da sexualidade formuladas por Judith Butler para explorar as possibilidades radicais destas personagens intrigantes, com o propósito de oferecer uma nova perspetiva sobre este romance clássico de Sá-Carneiro.

PALAVRAS-CHAVE. Portugal, Sá-Carneiro, modernismo, género, sexualidade, pós-estruturalismo.

'A fabulous speck on the Earth's surface': Depictions of Colonial Macao in 1950s' Hollywood

RUI LOPES

ABSTRACT. Macao was featured in over a dozen Hollywood productions while under Portugal's domination, most of which were released in the 1950s. Drawing on multi-archival research, film studies and postcolonial theory, this article contextualizes the colony's screen presence before examining three high-profile productions: *Macao* (1952), *Soldier of Fortune* (1955), and *Love is a Many-Splendored Thing* (1955), the latter two enabling a comparison with depictions of British rule in Hong Kong. The article contributes to the study of the international image of Portugal's empire, concluding that Macao's historical and geographical characteristics, as well as Hollywood's orientalist conventions and hyperbolic sense of spectacle, ended up conjuring an overall image of 'subaltern colonialism'.

KEYWORDS. Cinema, colonialism, Hollywood, Macao, orientalism, Portugal.

RESUMO. Macau apareceu em mais de uma dúzia de produções de Hollywood durante a dominação portuguesa, a maioria distribuída nos anos 50. Partindo de pesquisa em diversos arquivos, estudos fílmicos e teoria pós-colonial, este artigo contextualiza a presença cinematográfica dessa colónia e examina três grandes produções: *Macao* (1952), *Soldier of Fortune* (1955) e *Love is a Many-Splendored Thing* (1955), as duas últimas permitindo comparações com a representação do colonialismo britânico em Hong Kong. O artigo contribui para o estudo da imagem internacional do império português, concluindo que as características histórico-geográficas de Macau, bem como as convenções orientalistas e o hiperbólico sentido de espetáculo de Hollywood, projetaram uma imagem de 'colonialismo subalterno'.

PALAVRAS-CHAVE. Cinema, colonialismo, Hollywood, Macau, orientalismo, Portugal.

Censored and Banned: Portuguese Films during the Government of Marcello Caetano (1968–74)

ANA BELA MORAIS

ABSTRACT. This study examines the way that the censorship of Portuguese films operated during the government of Marcello Caetano (late 1968 to 1974). To do this it asks particular questions. For example, which themes were most often censored? How many films were censored, and how many completely banned, and why? Does the early period of the Caetano government show a relaxation in relation to what could be shown in Portuguese cinemas? These are some of the questions posed in order to facilitate a broader understanding of this period of Portuguese history.

KEYWORDS. Censorship, Portuguese cinema, Marcello Caetano, Portuguese Estado Novo (New State), mentalities.

RESUMO. Através do estudo da censura exercida ao cinema português, no tempo de Marcello Caetano (finais de 1968-1974), pretendo estudar o modo como era censurada a cinematografia nacional: quais os temas mais censurados? Quantos filmes foram censurados e quantos foram mesmo proibidos e porquê? Será que no início do governo marcelista houve uma abertura em relação ao que era permitido mostrar no cinema português? Estas são algumas perguntas para as quais este estudo procurará encontrar possíveis respostas, que possam ajudar a uma compreensão mais alargada desse período da história portuguesa.

PALAVRAS-CHAVE. Censura, cinema português, Marcello Caetano, Estado Novo português, mentalidades.

www.ingramcontent.com/pod-product-compliance
Lightning Source LLC
Chambersburg PA
CBHW061419300426
44114CB00015B/1994